Ada® for multi-microprocessors

Ada for multi-microprocessors

Edited by

MIKE TEDD

SPL International, Abingdon, UK,
and the University College of Wales, Aberystwyth.

STEFANO CRESPI-REGHIZZI

TXT, Milan, Italy,
and the Politecnico di Milano.

ANTONIO NATALI

CISE, Segrate, Italy,
and the University of Bologna.

The right of the
University of Cambridge
to print and sell
all manner of books
was granted by
Henry VIII in 1534.
The University has printed
and published continuously
since 1584.

Published on behalf of
the Commission of the European Communities by
CAMBRIDGE UNIVERSITY PRESS
Cambridge
London New York New Rochelle
Melbourne Sydney

Published by the Press Syndicate of the University of Cambridge
The Pitt Building, Trumpington Street, Cambridge CB2 1RP
32 East 57th Street, New York, NY 10022, USA
10 Stamford Road, Oakleigh, Melbourne 3166, Australia

First published 1984

Printed in Great Britain at the University Press, Cambridge

Library of Congress catalogue card number

ISBN 0 521 301033

Document No. EUR 9418 of the
Commission of the European Communities,
Directorate-General Information Market
and Innovation, Luxembourg

LEGAL NOTICE

Contents

Contributors

This book is largely derived from the final report of a study conducted over the period July 1982 to March 1983 by a team from:
- TXT SpA, Milano, Italy, the principal contractor,
- CISE, Segrate, Italy, and
- SPL International, Abingdon, UK.

integrated with a contribution on reliability and extensibility by the Ada UK Multiprocessor Subgroup (AMPSG), and with the presentation of the Italian pilot project MML (Multi-microprocessor line). These form chapters 8 and 9 respectively.

The original team included the following people:

TXT : A.Dapra, S.Gatti, S.Crespi-Reghizzi (also of the Politecnico di Milano);

CISE : F.Maderna, D.Belcredi, A.Natali (also of the University of Bologna);

SPL : R.A.Stammers, M.D.Tedd (also of the University College of Wales, Aberystwyth).

The main contributors to the AMPSG chapter were A.Cullen (of CASE), J.Hicks (of Ferranti), A.Hughes (of Marconi Research), M.Futcher (of FCSL), R.Hull (of the University of Sussex), and T.Moreton (of ITT). A.Hughes combined and edited the individual contributions of subgroup members.

The revising and editing which led to this book
was done by M.D.Tedd, S.Crespi-Reghizzi, and A.Natali.

The report and the book owe a great deal to the
comments of too many people to mention; the comments of the
Ada Europe Computer Integrated Manufacturing group were
especially valuable. One person who must be singled out is
J.Nissen, the responsible member of the series Editorial
Board; every part of the book has been improved as a result
of his efforts.

The study and the book could not have happened
without the support of the Information Technology Task Force
of the Commission of the European Communities. We are
pleased to acknowledge this support, and in particular the
help and encouragement of M.W.Rogers.

MDT, SC-R, AN.
July 1984.

1

Introduction

1.1 BACKGROUND

Industrial automation relies more and more on distributed multi-microprocessor hardware. There are several motivations for employing multiple-microprocessor systems:

- Distribution. It is often desirable to put the processing closer to the hardware it is controlling or monitoring.
- Flexibility. It should be easier to upgrade a system to handle a greater load by adding processors, rather than by replacing existing processors by larger ones.
- Modularity. The fact that a system is distributed encourages a modular approach to design. This leads to easier design, implementation, and maintenance.
- Predictability. It is much easier to predict the behaviour of a system when each part of it is performing a few tasks, than when a single processor is sharing its attentions over many tasks.
- Reliability. A system composed of multiple processors may be able to continue in some, probably degraded, fashion when one of its components fails.
- Cost-effectiveness. Modern microprocessors are cheap and have substantial, but limited, power. To achieve more total power means using much more expensive mini or mainframe computers, or

deploying numbers of microprocessors.
- Fault-tolerance. The existence of multiple
  processors means greater opportunities for making
  the system more tolerant of errors and faults.

The typical multi-microprocessor system consists
of a number of microprocessors in a network, cooperating to
perform a predefined set of computing tasks. The computing
activity of the system includes interactions with the
application environment and internal activities required for
exchanging information between processors, monitoring the
status of the network, and taking recovery action in
failures or emergencies. Where the application systems are
made of well-identified subsystems, the functions of each
subsystem are often allocated to a dedicated processor.

Families of hardware modules for constructing such
multi-micro systems are commercially available. The same
cannot be said of the software to support the development of
such systems.

The Ada language was designed for the US
Department of Defense, for programming embedded military
systems. Such systems have a great deal in common with
industrial real-time systems, so it is natural to expect Ada
to be suitable for programming these industrial systems.

1.2 THE EUROPEAN COMMISSION FUNDED STUDY

The primary input to this book has been the final
report of a study entitled "A Feasibility Study to Determine
the Applicability of Ada and Apse in a Multi-microprocessor
Distributed Environment" (TXT et al. 1983). This study was
undertaken over the period July 1982 to March 1983, by the
Italian companies TXT and CISE, and the British software
house SPL International.

The Italian companies have substantial experience
in industrial computer systems, and have worked together on
the MML system for programming distributed target
architectures. SPL has substantial experience of Ada and
its support environments.

The study was sponsored by the Commission of the European Communities, under their Multi-Annual Data Processing Programme.

The study addressed the following areas:
- analysis of typical industrial applications for multi-microprocessors;
- identification of the requirements placed on the programming language and associated support tools;
- study of the suitability of Ada and its support tools (the Apse), in the light of these requirements;
- strategies for developing the software for distributed systems;
- detailed study of the implications of this approach for the construction system (the software toolset that supports the development of the applications software system, and prepares binary images ready to be run in the target system).

It should be emphasised that this was an Ada study. We concentrated on those problems of distributed systems that arise out of the nature of Ada and its support environments, rather than on problems of distributed systems that arise whatever the chosen programming language(s). Thus the study did not address questions such as protocols for inter-processor communication, the handling of distributed databases, or the many aspects of reliability and extensibility in distributed systems. Other authors have studied language-independent problems (e.g. Liskov 1982).

The issues of reliability and extensibility have been the subject of study by the Multiprocessor Subgroup of Ada UK (AMPSG). They have contributed chapter 8 of this book.

1.3 CONTENTS OF THIS BOOK

Chapter 2 describes several examples of industrial real-time systems, drawn from the experience of TXT and CISE. It is recognised that most of these systems are relatively small. The chapter also discusses the general characteristics of the hardware and software architecture of such systems, and summarises various aspects of the examples in two tables.

In Chapter 3, we describe the requirements that these applications place on the programming language and on the software tools used to construct the systems.

Chapter 4 turns to consideration of Ada and its support environment, the Apse. We study how the features of the language relate to the requirements identified in Chapter 3, and how the Apse designs measure up in the same way. Neither Ada nor Apse have been designed with distributed targets in mind, and a major part of the chapter discusses the problems that arise from this.

Chapter 5 studies several possible strategies for the development of distributed systems in Ada; it is desirable to find an approach that does not change the language nor unduly restrict the way it is used.

One approach emerges as the most natural: the virtual node approach, where the designer is required to cluster tightly coupled Ada tasks into "virtual nodes". Communication between distinct virtual nodes is restricted to rendezvous, while tasks belonging to the same virtual node can also share data.

Other researchers studying distributed systems have introduced similar concepts, such as guardians (Liskov 1982), and zones (Downes and Goldsack 1980).

In Chapters 6 and 7, we consider in detail the construction system that would be necessary to support the development, in Ada, of software systems to run on distributed targets. Chapter 6 concentrates on identifying the issues to be tackled; one such issue is describing the target hardware so that the construction system can automatically create object programs for the chosen configuration.

Chapter 7 concentrates on the implications for the
Apse toolset, in terms of probable modifications that would
be needed to existing tools, what new tools would be needed,
and what information the user would need to supply to the
construction system.

Chapter 8, the AMPSG chapter, studies the topics
of reliability and extensibility in distributed systems.   It
first identifies requirements in these areas, and discusses
possible approaches.   The details of various approaches are
considered, separating out approaches that are independent
of Ada, and those that relate directly to Ada.   Finally, the
problems of dynamic upgrading and reconfiguration are
examined.

The proposed approach contains several ideas from
the MML ("multi-micro-line") language and its support
environment MMDS ("multi-micro-development system"), which
are described in Boari et al. (1982b and 1984).   These
projects have tackled the problems arising from distributed
targets and changing hardware configuration for MML, a
language much simpler than Ada.   The experience of the
Italian companies in developing MML and MMDS are reported in
Chapter 9.

2

Examples of distributed systems

2.1 INTRODUCTION

In this chapter, we present brief overviews of
several existing projects involving distributed systems.
The requirements arising from these systems are discussed in
chapter 3. Note that most of these systems are relatively
small.

"Distributed system" is a general term covering
very different cases, from tiny multi-microprocessors to
geographically distinct mainframes. Size and cost are two
discriminating parameters, but architecture is an equally
important one. This is considered in 2.2, where
architectures (hardware and software) are grouped into
classes, based on interprocessor communication and operating
system support.

2.2 TARGET SYSTEM ARCHITECTURES

2.2.1 Hardware Architectures

Probably the most important characterisation of a
distributed architecture is the means of communication
between processors. In this respect, it is customary to
distinguish tightly coupled, and loosely coupled systems.

In a tightly coupled system, the processors
communicate via a shared memory, which may be dual (or
multiple) port, or on a global bus, or an intermediate
multi-level scheme like TOMP (Conte 1981).

In a loosely coupled system, the processors
communicate by links, which may be point-to-point lines
(serial or parallel), local area networks (e.g. Ethernet,

Cambridge ring), or long haul (wide area) networks.

Much of the study is devoted to tightly coupled architectures, which we consider promising for industrial applications. Notice also that in more complex architectures, several clusters of tightly coupled processors can be loosely coupled. Long haul distributed systems are not considered, although in principle nothing prevents application of our study to them too. Typical wide area networks consist of (large) autonomous computers; the rather monolithic view of the system taken in this study is not appropriate in that case.

Using the great variety of commercially available boards, it is possible to implement a distributed system tailored to specific needs. Indeed it is often possible to use more than one kind of link (common bus, double-port memory, serial/parallel links, local networks) obtaining complex architectures involving both tight and loose connections; in such a system, attention must be paid to the needs of inter-task communications.

If there is no need for fast computation or other specific requirements, the processors in a system will usually be all of the same kind ("homogeneous").

2.2.2 Software Architectures

Aspects relevant here are the kind of operating system or kernel, and whether each computer has the same operating system. Language issues are also important. Schematically, three kinds of run-time support could be considered:

a) a multi-tasking kernel (e.g. Intel's RMX, TXT's ZEX, SPL's SMT);

b) a general purpose real-time operating system (e.g. Digital's RSX);

c) a periodical monitor, as used in avionics systems to schedule execution of tasks.

Case a) is central to our study: typically each microprocessor in the system will run under control of a kernel supporting the execution of Ada tasks.

Case b) is attractive for more complex local-area like systems. Often, a type a) application is written in a single language, whereas type b) applications could consist of several packages written in different languages. The specific problems of interfacing different languages and operating systems are not addressed by this study.

Case c) is not considered; it is specialised, and would impose severe restrictions on the use of Ada tasking.

2.3 SURVEY OF APPLICATIONS

2.3.1 Manufacturing Automation

This broad industrial sector encompasses all kinds of automation tasks from parts fabrication, to assembly, inspection packing and storage. Complexity of digital control equipment ranges greatly from simple PLC to large mainframe computers. In the more advanced automated factories several levels of control are integrated, from single machine-shop numerical control to management information systems. We shall limit ourselves to the lower levels of control, which are relevant to this study; production planning, optimisation and management information systems are not covered.

Example 1: Hydraulic Press

The purpose is to form metal sheets by stretching. Sheets are manually loaded into two holding clamps and stretched onto a mould, up to yielding point, by a coordinated movement of clamps and mould holder. Clamps and mould have an oscillatory and linear motion. Motion is obtained for each clamp or mould by a pair of cylinders with speed and position control, conceptually similar to a stepping motor. Two modes of operation are required:
- on-line: execution of machine cycles predefined during an off-line phase, or recorded on cassette;

- off-line: preparation of machine cycles to be
optionally stored on cassette.

The system structure is that of a master
microprocessor and three slaves (Figure 2.1).   Information
flow between slaves is restricted to emergency interrupts.

The system functions are:
- choice of on-line versus off-line,
- handler of off-line commands,
- definition and storage of machine cycles via
keyboard,
- synchronisation between master and slaves,
- execution of machine cycles,
- keyboard and machine status display handlers,
- file system and cassette driver.

The hardware components of the system are
commercially available 8-bit single board computers, and
peripherals which are operator console, video terminal,
cassette, and the plant peripherals; these are 85 digital
inputs for plungers and selectors, 56 digital inputs for
alarms and diagnostic signals, 40 digital outputs for light
signals and actuator, (electric-valve) controls, and 12
lines for controlling the movements of the press.

Fault tolerance:- Auto-diagnostic programs are
automatically executed during idle periods. Fault symptoms
cause an alarm and stop the machine.   CPU activities of
master and slaves are controlled by a watch-dog timer
periodically reset by system routines.   In addition slaves
are checked by the master using time-outs at each
information exchange.

User interaction:-
- interactive definition of machine cycles,
- semi-automatic control of speed and position of
actuators via thumb wheels,
- manual control of actuators,
- display of press status.

Speed:- The system must service interrupts with a
frequency of 570 Hz.

Physical distribution:- Processes are contiguous.

Logical relations between processes:- As each
slave controls an actuator, they have to cooperate, through
the coordination of the master. In addition the latter
performs other tasks: control of operator panel, video
terminal, and cassette. The master issues commands to
slaves. A command must be completed before a new command to
the same slave can be issued. The situation can be compared
to a very simple producer/consumer relation.

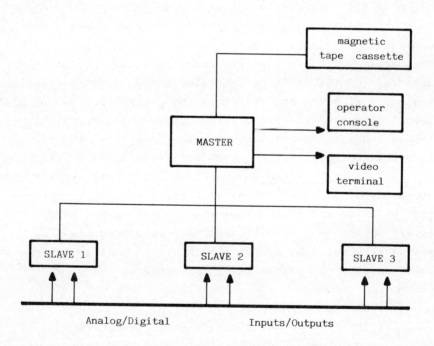

Figure 2.1 Hydraulic press control system

Example 2: Control System for Thermoforming Machines

The purpose of this system is thermal forming of plastic sheets. Sheets of plastic material are picked up from the stock, one at time, by several suction devices and are then centred by pistons connected to a centering device, and successively grasped by the clamps fixed on the transfer mechanism. Meanwhile, sheets in the pre-heating and heating stations are heat treated, and the sheet in the forming station is thermoformed. The sheets are held in position by six frames which are also grasped by clamps mounted on the translation mechanism. At the end of the forming process the frames open and the entire transfer trolley advances, taking the new sheet to the pre-heating station, the final heated sheet to the forming station, and the formed sheet to the ejection station. At the end of the transfer trolley's forward travel, the frames close, clamping the sheets, and the heating and forming operations are started. The clamps then open and the trolley moves backwards. When the trolley returns to its initial position, a new sheet is fed in, the clamps close again and the process restarts.

The system structure (Fig 2.2) is tightly coupled, with a master microprocessor and a slave, connected via a dual port memory.

The system peripherals are:- command peripherals: keyboard display terminal, and magnetic tape cassette; process peripherals: controllers of 120 heating elements, and temperature regulation of the 9 zones of the heating elements.

The system functions are:
- management of the machine operation cycle, alarms and anomalies,
- management of the forming cycle,
- operator/machine interface during the program editing phase,
- data exchanges between master and slave microprocessors,

- file system-magnetic tape cassette driver,
- synchronisation between master and slave,
- temperature regulation of the 9 zones of the
  heating elements,
- control of the 120 heating elements of the final
  heating stations.

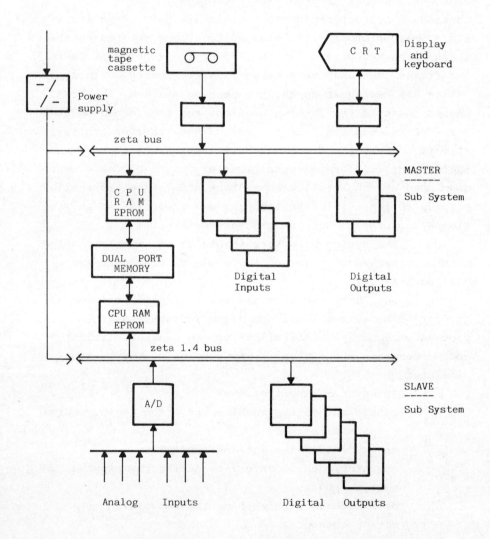

Figure 2.2   Thermoforming system

The hardware components of the system are as
follows. Boards are based on Intel 8085 processors. The
system is made up of the following functional units:
- central units (master and slave),
- RAM/EPROM storage unit,
- input-output cards with galvanic separation,
- magnetic tape cassette interface,
- display terminal interface,
- analog-digital converter,
- multiplexer for analog signals coming from the
  thermocouples,
- output board for controlling the heating elements
  of the preheating and heating stations.

Fault tolerance:- On detection of an anomaly, the
system stops. Alarms and anomalies are signalled by
messages appearing on the monitor and sometimes by audio
alarms. The operator has a push button to acknowledge and,
if necessary, to silence alarms. Special sequences are
included to ensure maximum machine safety.

Type of user interaction:- The parameters of the
mould to be employed are stored on magnetic tape. After
starting up the system, the operator need only recall from a
magnetic tape the specific data on the item to be produced
and actuate the online operation of the equipment. After
this command is transmitted from the video terminal the
machine starts until it is stopped by the operator or until
an anomaly occurs.

Example 3: Control System for a Bottling Line

The purpose of this system is to control a
bottling line, coordinating the various machines positioned
along the length of carrying belt. The aim of the system is
to maximise production (up to 10,000 bottles/hour) and to
decrease bottle breakages. The coordination activity must
take into account the possible failures and/or emergencies
and must control the speed of the machines. As a secondary
purpose, the system must acquire production data (bottle

number, stop intervals etc.) which must be stored and
displayed on request. The structure of the bottling line is
described in Figure 2.3.

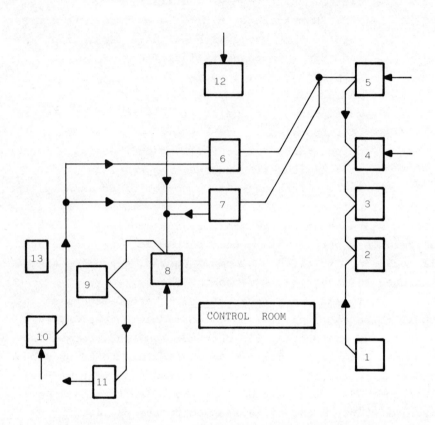

Figure 2.3 General structure of a bottling line

The system structure is shown in Figure 2.4. It
includes a central processing unit (CPU) and as many
peripheral units (PPUs) as machines to be coordinated (13 in
our case). The CPU is also connected to a console (board +
printer) and operates a synoptic panel. The CPU and PPU are
linked by a serial line. The PPUs are located near the
machine to be controlled, while the CPU and peripheral units
are located in another room. All the PPUs are polled at
fixed intervals by the CPU.

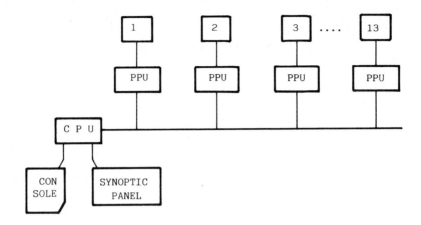

Figure 2.4   Bottling line control system

Central unit functions:
- interaction with the operator through the system console,
- interaction with the PPUs through a linkage line,
- acquisition of production data from the bottle-pass sensors,
- check of line start-up conditions,
- starting and controlling speed of all the machines,
- monitoring anomalies.

Peripheral unit functions:
- control a single machine operation,
- show the machine status on CPU request,
- set the machine speed on CPU order,
- detect possible malfunction of a single machine.

The hardware components of the system are these. The central unit and the 13 peripheral units are based on an 8-bit SBC with I/O and serial interface. There can be up to 16 peripheral units. A keyboard (with printer) and a front panel are connected to the system.

Fault tolerance:- The system must continue (reduced) operation in the presence of faulty PPUs.

Type of user interaction:- The operator interacts
with the system by START/STOP commands. Also, by using the
keyboard, the operator can ask for a production data
printout, but only after the system is stopped.

Speed:- Peripheral units are polled every 100
msec.

Physical distribution:- The machines to be
controlled are distributed over an area of 50 - 100 metres.
The room housing the central unit is 70 metres from the
farthest machine.

Logical relation between processes:- The machines
are sequentially related.

2.3.2 Data Acquisition Systems

Because of its low cost and reprogramming
flexibility, the microcomputer is also used in many data
acquisition and measurement systems. Typically several
microcomputers are tied to a minicomputer, which performs
larger data manipulation and analysis tasks.

Processing, which used to be concentrated, is now
dispersed to the local level. The effect of all this is to
improve the quality of data obtained, and speed up its
acquisition. We briefly describe two examples of data
acquisition systems using a "mixed" architecture (mini +
micro). The mini could now be replaced by a 16 bit micro
having the essential software tools (operating system,
compiler, file system, etc.).

Example 4: Multiprocessor System for Data Acquisition for Creep Fatigue and Environment Fatigue Test

The purpose of this system is research on the
behaviour of stressed metallic material.

The system functions are:

During creep fatigue testing, a sample of metallic
material is introduced into an oven and deformed over a
widely variable period of time (1 sec to several hours).

The system periodically acquires the following
parameters: the load (P) and displacement (J) of the sample,
the piston displacement, and the applied piston control
function, derived from the function generator; the frequency
of sampling this data is inversely proportional to the cycle
period. Another quantity sampled is the temperature in
three distinct points of the machine at intervals of about
30 seconds.

The system provides for alarms and, during every
cycle, computes some limited functions on data collected.

During environment fatigue testing the pre-
engraved sample is introduced into a pressurised vat (150
atm, 300 C) or into a water bath (100 C) and submitted to a
strain by a piston controlled by the system. The system
acquires the same parameters as in the creep example.

Other parameters sampled are sample temperature,
and (every ten seconds) water flow for pressurised vat or
water temperature (4 points) for water bath.

The mass of records produced by the acquisition
processes is stored on a hard disk. Files containing data
acquired or computed during every cycle must be available
during the whole test (up to six months), for off-line
computation. At the end of the testing phase all the data
will be stored on permanent archives.

The system structure consists of:
- seven acquisition points for creep fatigue testing
- three acquisition points for environment fatigue
  testing
- one acquisition point for plant parameters (analog
  signals concerning the pressurised vat water
  circuit: pressure, conductivity, acidity, oxygen
  concentration, etc.).

The acquisition points are connected via serial
interfaces, to two microprocessors (concentrators), which
are connected to a minicomputer (coordinator) (see Fig 2.5).

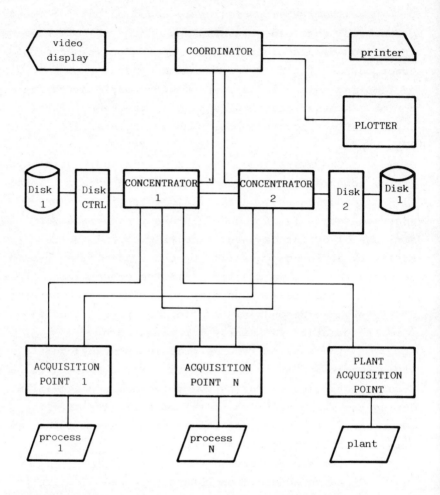

Figure 2.5:   Creep and fatigue system overview

The hardware components of the system are two 8
bit microprocessors (Z8Ø), and a Data General Nova4
minicomputer. The microprocessor concentrators handle the
hard disk file system, and supervise the acquisition points.
The minicomputer coordinator interfaces with the operator,
processes acquired data, and drives the printer, plotter,
and floppy disk.

Fault tolerance:- The system is partly duplicated
to improve the MTBF. It has two hard disk controllers and

two concentrators. If a concentrator goes offline for
maintenance or repair the coordinator can transfer data to
the remaining one. The system can work in degraded
situations.

Speed:- The highest frequency of sampling for
every acquisition point is 256 samples/second x 4 inputs,
(1024 samples/second).

Example 5: Inspection and Testing

The purpose of this system is to carry out
automatic line inspections and tests on washing machines. It
consists of a "Central Unit" which collects data from a
number of "Line Units" which in turn collect data from a
number of "Testing Stations". Each line unit is positioned
at the end of an assembly line. Testing stations move along
the line with the machine under test. They collect test
data, store it in a buffer and at the end of the line
transmit the data to the line unit via an infra-red
input/output system.

The system structure is that of a multimicro
system having a microcomputer for the central unit, one for
each line unit and one for each testing station.

The system functions are:

The line unit:

- acquires the test results from testing stations,
- prints the contents slip to be attached to the
  washing machine,
- transmits test data statistics to the central
  unit,
- displays the testing pattern and notifies
  anomalies.

Each testing station:

- measures the current consumption and water loaded
  and discharged by the washing machine,

- communicates with the operator (display-operator panel),
- processes the collected data,
- drives the digital outputs (remote control switches, electro-mechanical valves etc.),
- transmits test data and possible failure codes to the line unit.

The hardware components are as follows. The system is built around Intel 8085 microprocessors. It is composed of:

- CPU (Central Processor, line units, testing stations),
- memory expansion (EPROM + RAM),
- optoisolated input output,
- infra-red serial interface,
- voltage/frequency converter,
- display,
- operator panel,
- parallel interface (in the line unit, for collecting alarm signals from the assembly line),
- serial I/O interface current loop (for connecting line unit to central unit).

Fault tolerance:- The line units have a watch dog mechanism. They also enable a time-out for printing operations, and serial communication with testing stations. The EPROMS are auto-checked during the idle phases of the systems.

User interaction:- The user interacts with the system in conversational mode.

Physical distribution:- The processes are locally distributed around the plant.

Logical relation between processes:- The testing stations collect data and transmit them to the line unit in a producer-consumer mode. The same model can be applied to line-unit central unit relation.

Example 6: Nuclear Reactor Cooling Circuit
Multiprocessor Data Acquisition System

The purpose of this system is the study of
thermodynamic conditions in a nuclear reactor cooling
circuit. The system must acquire about two hundred analog
signals and controls several outputs to the plant. It must
be placed as near as possible to the plant to minimise noise
on sampled signals. The operator is remote because of
dangerous environmental conditions.

The system structure is shown in Figure 2.6.
Because of large amounts of data, and high acquisition
frequency, the system shares its functions between a
microcomputer and a mini.

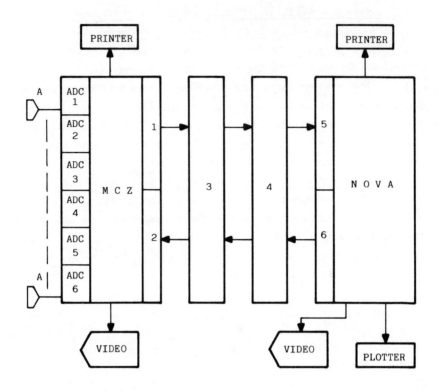

A : Amplifiers   1,2: CISE MCZ boards
3,4: Interfaces for optoisolated line   5,6: CISE Nova boards

Figure 2.6: Reactor cooling circuit data acquisition system

The system functions are as follows. The
microcomputer samples analog data, processes data acquired,
and partially controls the plant in case of alarm. Data
sampled is sent in parallel on optoisolated lines. The mini
stores the data on a nine track tape (1.5 Megabytes
capacity). Data computations are made off-line by the
minicomputer.

The hardware components of the system consist of
Zilog MCZ/20 and a set of dedicated special purpose boards,
and of a general purpose mini (Data General Nova3).

Fault tolerance is not required because tests are
short and easily repeated.

Type of user interaction:- conversational.

Speed:- The frequency of data acquisition is about 20,000 samples/second.

Physical distribution:- The micro must be close to the plant. The mini is located in another room.

2.3.3 Power Distribution

Example 7: Control System for a Spot-welding Line

The purpose of this system is to handle welding requests arriving from a certain number (< 30) of welders, in order not to exceed the scheduled power consumption. The two main advantages are better welding quality, and power saving.

The system structure (Fig 2.7) includes one central processing unit (CPU) connected to a variable number of peripheral processing units (PPUs) through a suitable connection line (serial bus). Three welding machines are linked to each peripheral station and the central unit controls an operators panel.

Central unit functions:-
- input of the system configuration data from the operating panel and system initialisation,
- control of interaction with the peripheral units,
- operation of the available feeding resources and control of their limits.

In the initialisation stage, the CPU automatically identifies the system taking into account how many peripheral units are connected. Afterwards the CPU periodically questions the PPUs, acquires the "state" of the various welders and controls power assignment. Depending on the "state" of the welders (acquired by the peripheral units), the CPU carries out certain specific actions.

Peripheral unit functions:- The peripheral unit, interfaced with the welders, performs:

- initialisation: reading the switches that
  determine the characteristics of the welders
  (maximum power consumption, type of connection to
  the power source), etc.,
- reading the input line to determine the welder
  state (welding request, welding under way, welding
  end, etc.),
- control of interaction with the central unit,
- sending OK to the welders.

The maximum number of PPU lines (each controlling
3 welders) is 16.

The hardware components of the system are a
central unit based on a Z-80 SBC and peripheral units for
which suitable hardware has been developed based on Intel's
8048. There are from 2 to 16 8-bit processors. There is a
control panel fitted with selectors.

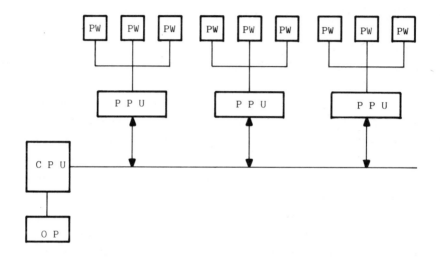

CPU = Central Processing Unit   PW = Pinch Welders
PPU = Peripheral Processing Unit   OP = Operator Panel

Figure 2.7:   Control system structure for a welding line

    Fault tolerance:- The system must be protected
from communication line noises. It must continue to work in
the presence of one or more faulty PPUs (reduced operation
capability).

    Type of user interaction:- The interaction with
the operator occurs only during initialisation by setting
certain parameters through the selectors. Welder
characteristics are always defined during the initialisation

phase.

Speed:- The system is undemanding; any input line corresponds to a button pushed by the welding operator. The peripheral units are polled at intervals of 100 msec.

Physical distribution:- The welders under control are 50 to 100 metres away.

Logical relation between processes:- The processes under control (the welders) are absolutely independent, except for the use of electric power, which, in this case, is a common resource.

Example 8: A Telecontrol System for Electric Power Production and Distribution

The purpose of this telecontrol system under development is to receive data from several power stations, to check for agreement of measurements with limit values, notify the operator, to forward alarms to higher decision centres, to receive orders from the operator, and to send back telecommands to the power station. The estimated software effort is 140 man-years.

The system structure is that of a set of processors interconnected by a duplicated token-passing local area network. Processors are of two kinds: up to 15 multi-microprocessors (based on the Digital J-11), and one PDP-11. Peripherals include many lines, VDUs, disc, and alarm panel.

The central PDP-11 handles a database containing the description of the power stations, logs events, etc. Graphic packages display the schemes of power stations, and their actual parameters. Another software package handles operator dialogues, using syntax directed techniques.

Functions of microcomputers:- The multi-microcomputers are connected to the remote power stations by slow telegraph lines, and check received measurements against nominal values, or dispatch telecommands to the stations. A stand-by is available to replace faulty units. One microcomputer forwards important information and alarms to higher decision centres.

On each processor, there is a local, multi-task, real-time operating system. Application tasks are coded in Fortran.

Fault tolerance:- As mentioned, there is a database on a PDP-11, which is partially replicated on each microprocessor for the power stations it has to control. The database can be modified during normal operation, and the new copy must be tested for consistency before replacing the old one, without disturbing normal operations. The operator unit is duplicated (hot spare) and manages the man-machine interface. All data traffic within the system goes through a duplicated node, which verifies that a task has the right to call another one, and that answers are sent back. Testing and diagnostic packages monitor the functioning of the system.

2.3.4 Continuous Process Control

Instead of detailing specific examples, an attempt is made to outline the basic features of continuous control applications.

These systems have quite different characteristics because of the variety of processes to be controlled (chemical, thermal, electrical, etc.), the different size of the plants and the environmental conditions. It is possible to find analogies between different systems, but in some cases their classification depends on the kind of application (e.g. chemical), in other cases on the function supplied (control loop, controlled signals, algorithms used, etc.). These systems are often designed and produced just for one or a few applications and sometimes they are obtained from a reconfiguration of an existing system. Software readability, maintainability and valid maintenance support during a long project life-cycle are perhaps the main requirements for this class of application.

The response time required is dependent on the process being controlled: mechanical processes require fast response to asynchronous events (about 100 microseconds),

while thermal systems are much less critical. Data
acquisition and processing functions are usually more time-
consuming because of non-intelligent peripheral devices.

System complexity depends on the following
parameters: kind of action on the plant, from the simple
on/off policy up to the generation of complex analogic
functions, frequency of actions on the plant, number of
controlled devices, number of variables involved in the
control loop and their interaction, and complexity of
control algorithm (from p.i.d. up to recursive algorithms).

In the most simple cases the actions emulate a
"relay logic". They simply repeat a sequential algorithm
based solely on boolean operations (and, or,...).

Fault tolerance:- The on-off control system is
mostly used. Multiplication of hardware and software
components is often preferred to error detection and
recovery methods (both hardware and software). Every action
on the plant is performed only when all the systems
controlling the same device give their consent; the systems
are synchronised only at critical points.

In many cases security rules or legal requirements
insist that the final "actuator" is a human. Sometimes mini
or micro control systems are used together with discrete
systems. In any case the most critical activities are data
acquisition, performing control algorithms, and controlling
actuators. Less critical is plant and user parameter
updating. See Randell et al. (1978).

User interaction:- Process control applications
require stand-alone systems able to work for a long time
without any human intervention. This is particularly true
for "black-box" systems that act on a particular piece of
plant. On the other hand there are many systems that
require a friendly user interface both for supervision and
parameter manipulation. The software interface is thus a
major part of the total system software; user/system
interfaces are becoming more and more sophisticated: graphic
terminals and functional keyboards are largely used instead
of switches, leds, numerical display.

System architecture:-

Because of the wide range of applications, many different types of computing units may be used: PLC, microprocessors, minicomputers.

The monoprocessor architectures vary from simple ROM-based microprocessor systems up to minicomputers; multiple processor architectures are usually hybrid (one or more microcomputers connected to a mini).

Minicomputer-based systems often have mass storage and are used both for software development and online applications; microprocessors need a separate development system (host-target approach). Many commercially available software libraries are useful on minicomputer-based systems.

Usually the minicomputer has far more computing power than its application requires, but nevertheless it is preferred to the micro for the following reasons:

- availability of packages and operating systems,
- it can be used also for program development,
- systems based on microprocessors do not have readily available development tools that are cost-effective and reliable,
- no integrated multi-micro-processor system development tools are available.

Languages and operating systems:-

For microprocessor-based systems assembly language is heavily used for programming I/O, interrupt handling etc. High level languages, usually supplied by the microprocessor manufacturer, are also used; the run-time support is also manufacturer supplied, or internally designed to fit particular requirements or to introduce additional features.

In minicomputer-based systems assembly language is still often adopted despite the availability of high level languages, such as Pearl or RTL/2. The supplied real-time operating system is usually used. It should be noticed that available concurrent programming languages are rarely used, and distributed systems are not common. Furthermore even if a high-level language is used, the programmer must often deal with low level details, lacking effective tools such as symbolic debuggers.

SPL makes extensive use of RTL/2 for process
control systems. Also, for large applications, a package
called CASCADE is employed. As well as modules to help with
functions like control loops and colour graphics, it
provides an engineer-oriented plant control language (PCL)
used to write the bulk of any particular system.

Development system:- For micro software
development, the methods used are those already described in
other sections. For minicomputers, software development is
normally carried out on the target system itself, or on a
larger configuration of the same computer.

In summary, the following needs can be identified
for process control applications:

- high degree of flexibility and re-configurability;
- significant modularity: it should be possible to
  add to or subtract from the system with little or
  no effort;
- variable degree of fault tolerance or some form of
  graceful degradation;
- allocation of functions to different units;
- high local computation and little communication
  activity with the supervisor.

2.4 PROJECTS OVERVIEW

2.4.1 Introduction

The projects described in section 2.3 are analysed
in two ways. Various high level aspects are first discussed
and summarised. Then the hardware and software of the
applications are discussed and summarised in a table.

2.4.2 Analysis of Various High Level Aspects

In most of the systems we have described, the
project dimensions are modest; there are typically only two
programmers.

An evolution in programming languages can be seen.
At the beginning microprocessor programmers used to write

programs in assembler (ASM), but then they started to
utilise higher level languages. Most high level language
compilers for micros (Fortran, PL/M, PL/Z) were supplied by
microprocessor manufacturers.

For critical applications, with strong constraints
of time or storage, assembler is still used, but it has been
enriched with many structured programming constructs
(Structured Assembler /ASZ/).

Most applications described use real-time
multitasking operating systems. They are supplied by the
companies that supply the microprocessors or designed by the
system houses that supply the control system.

Dedicated tasks are designed for communication
between microprocessors.

Software is always developed by a host/target
approach. That is, a program that will execute in an
embedded target computer is developed on a host computer
which offers extensive support facilities.

Two different classes of host systems are in use:
a) Microprocessor Development Systems (MDS) supplied
   by the manufacturer.

These provide tools and facilities only for the
microprocessors supplied by the company and are generally
single-user.

b) A general purpose minicomputer used as a Universal
   Development System (UDS).

On a UDS, it is possible to use cross assemblers
and cross compilers for different kinds of microprocessors,
and to use the standard support packages for program
development (editors, file system, library manager) which
are generally more advanced than on MDS's. A multi-user
environment is necessary as the number or dimensions of
projects grow.

The debugging and testing phase is critical,
especially in multiprocessor environments, and it is often
more expensive than the development phase. Current practice
is to use few tools, often limited to a vendor-supplied
emulator plus perhaps a special purpose tool (environment

simulator). The tools available are not well integrated, nor do they form a complete set. Debugging tools for multiprocessing environments are almost totally nonexistent.

The delivery time is often short (under a year); this requires the availability of powerful and efficient development and testing tools, and invites the use of a high level language. The average life of the systems is 5 to 10 years, often determined by the life of the plant.

Modifications and system updates are larger and more frequent during the first months of life but are greatly reduced after the tuning phase.

Table 2.1 summarises some of the above aspects.

Ex. No.	No. of Progr- ammers	No. of Instruc- tions	Language	Man Year	Opsys	Develop- ment Approach	Deli- very Time	Life time yrs
1	3		PLM+ASZ	2	RMX/80	H-T(UDS)	2	5-10
2	3		PLM+ASZ	1.5	ZEX/I	H-T(UDS)	0.8	5
3	2		ASM	0.9	-	H-T(MDS)	0.8	5-10
4	2		ASM+PLZ*	5		H-T(MDS)	2.5	10
5	2	8500	PLM	2	ZEX/I	H - T	1	
6	2		ASM	1		H (MLZ)	1	7
7	2	2800	ASM	0.6		H-T(MDS)	0.6	5-10
8	30	90000	Fortran	140	RSX	H & H-T	3	10

(*) The minicomputer software was developed in Fortran

Table 2.1

2.4.3 Analysis of Application Hardware and Software

The proposed classification is derived from the applications described in the previous section but can be used as a guide for similar systems.

In each row of Table 2.2 below there is a set of possible values (key-words) mutually or not mutually exclusive. The use of these key-words is explained below.

a) Number of processors

The number of processing units present on the system. We exclude single-chip processors used to drive peripheral controllers.

b) Type of microprocessors

In this context we note only the word length of
the microprocessors used, either an 8 bit microprocessor
such as 8085, Z80, 6800, or a 16 bit microprocessor such as
8086, Z8000, 68000. (A 16-bit minicomputer is classified as
a microprocessor since today it would presumably be replaced
by a micro.)

c) Type of link between processors

The following common solutions are considered:-
Serial link: any kind of possible serial link (e.g. point-
to-point, multi-drop, serial bus). Parallel link:
identifies either a global parallel bus which can link more
than one master processor (e.g: Intel Multibus) or a special
purpose link using parallel I/O. Normally, in the first
case, the processors can access a global memory. Double
port memory: a simple and economic way to link two different
microcomputers (with local resources such as CPU, I/O,
memory) connecting two different buses; Local net, such as
Ethernet.

d) Types of peripherals

We distinguish different peripheral classes:

Command peripheral: identifies any peripheral used
by the operator to interact with the system, e.g: console
and/or video-terminals, control panels with switches, push-
buttons, selectors, potentiometers, synoptic panels (to
monitor the status of variables).

Process peripheral: rather than enumerate all
process peripherals (e.g. sensors, actuators), we quote the
number of I/O signals (analog inputs, analog outputs,
digital inputs, and digital outputs).

Auxiliary peripheral: we classify as auxiliary
peripherals both mass memory and printers.

e) Degree of fault tolerance

The fault tolerance requirements of a system have
a great influence on system complexity. It is not easy to
establish precisely the degree of fault tolerance required,
since we would need to consider many different parameters
(e.g. MTBF, availability, coverage). Here we indicate the

level of protection supported by the control system.

Fault detection: hardware and software mechanisms used to detect a fault.

Fault containment: techniques used to prevent fault-damaged information from propagating through a system after a fault, but before its detection.

Fault diagnosis: hardware and software techniques to locate and identify a fault.

Fault recovery: mechanisms called upon to correct the fault by "voting out" incorrect results or replacing faulty components with spares.

Graceful degradation: the system is not able to recover from a fault but there is only a partial functional degradation. Notice that a graceful degradation is normally simple to obtain in a distributed system, where damage in a peripheral processing unit does not cause global degradation.

f) Type of user interaction

From a logical point of view the user can interact with the system in many different ways (using the command peripheral indicated in d). We distinguish:

Start-stop: the user can only determine system start-up and shut-down.

Setting parameters: using a special purpose peripheral (such as a control panel) the operator sets some configuration parameters.

Conversational: using (normally) a terminal the user can input commands and parameters and the system can output various information concerning the status of the process under control. This form of interaction usually takes place concurrently with other system activities.

g) Logical relations between processes

The processes that form the system can be:

Independent: they have no logical relationship;

Interfering: they are usually independent but sometimes they access some common resource;

Cooperating: the processes cooperate closely to carry out a well defined task. The different forms of cooperation are not further analysed.

i) Type of program memory

We distinguish the systems as:

ROM-based: all application and system programs are stored in ROM. There is no need for mass memory to start up the system.

RAM-based: the application programs are stored in mass memory (usually some kind of disks). At system start up they are loaded (completely or partially) in RAM memory. A small read only memory usually contains the bootstrap loader.

l) Physical distribution of processes

A multi-micro system could be logically distributed but not physically distributed. Regarding the physical distribution we can have:

Local distribution: the system units are distributed in a small area (e.g: a building);

Geographic distribution: the processing units are in different geographic areas (cities, countries or continents);

Boxed: the processing units are in one box.

	1	2	3	5	4	6	7	8
number of processors	4	4	12	3 to ?	3	2	2to 16	1 to
type of micro processors	8 bit	8 bit	8 bit	8 bit	8 bit	8 bit	8 bit	16 bi
link type between processors	paral- lel link	dual port	serial link	port port	serial link	serial link	serial link	local net
command periphs.	video term.	video term.	consol synopt panel	video term.	video term.	video term.	oper- ator panel	video line
process periphs.	3	2	2	?	4	5	1	elect power dist.
auxiliary periphs.	181	129	13	?	11	6	?	
degree of fault- tolerance	detect	diagn	detect	detect	recov.	---	con- tain	conta recov
type of user interactn.	set param.	set param	set param.	conv.	conv.	conv.	start /stop	conve
processors logical relation	coop.	coop.	coop.	coop.	interf erence	interf erence	interf erence	coop. and inter
program memory	ROM	ROM	ROM	ROM	ROM	ROM	ROM	ROM/R
physical distribut.	boxed	boxed	local	local	local	local	local	loca

Table 2.2

3

Requirements for the programming language and tools

3.1 INTRODUCTION

Following the examples that we have given in the previous chapter, we can now describe the requirements that arise for the programming language and tools needed to construct such systems. We should again emphasise that the experience described above is biased towards relatively small systems; larger systems may well be more demanding in various respects, notably in program structure, and in fault handling and its implications for dynamic restructuring of the software system.

It is convenient to discuss separately the requirements for languages, the programming environment, and run-time aspects, although they are not entirely independent. For each stated requirement we shall explain the motivation and provide evidence of its feasibility.

The requirements of highly reliable systems were not covered by the original study; they are considered in Chapter 8.

Further motivation for choices having to do with distribution concurrency and input-output is found in Chapter 10, where we present the rationale for MML.

3.2 REQUIREMENTS FOR THE PROGRAMMING LANGUAGE

3.2.1 A modern, high level programming language

The motivation for this is to reduce the software
development and maintenance costs associated with assembly
languages.

Simplicity in learning and using the language, or
an effective subset, is an important characteristic, since
not all application engineers can be expected to be computer
science graduates. (Language simplicity is relatively less
important for larger systems than those we have considered;
most software for larger systems would be written by full-
time specialists.)

The feasibility is demonstrated by the large
numbers of industrial applications that have been programmed
using high-level languages such as Fortran, RTL-2, PLZ,
PL/M, and Pascal (Crespi-Reghizzi 1980, Boari 1982a). Even
single-chip microprocessors can now be programmed in high-
level languages.

Subsequent sections consider in detail the
following language requirements:
- program structure and modularity
- facilities for program development methodologies
- data types
- data structures
- assignments and expressions
- control structures
- processes, synchronisation and communication
- input-output
- exception handling

3.2.2 Program Structure and Modularity

Minimally, a program should be structured as a set
of separately compiled modules, as in assembly language
programs. However the use of interfaces between modules
should be checked.

The motivation here is to subdivide program
development, to separate data from code, and to provide

rudimentary facilities for encapsulation, and information
hiding, e.g. by providing abstract data types.

Multi-level nesting of procedures, packages, and
other program units, to hide inner details and for
protection, is useful but not essential, because of the
relatively simple program structures found in these
industrial automation projects.

In our experience it is convenient to be able to
create several instances of an abstract data type, which
differ by some parameters (e.g. to define identical
peripherals connected to different addresses). Handling this
problem by editing the source text for each instantiation
can lead to difficult maintenance problems if many people
are involved, and the software life-time is long. "Generic"
packages or conditional compilation provide an answer to
this problem.

3.2.3 Facilities for Development Methodologies

The future will see much more in the way of
reusable software modules, so "libraries" must be supported,
for top-down as well as bottom-up development. Top-down and
bottom-up design methodologies can already be accomplished
if the language provides separately compilable modules and
subprograms. However these methods are considerably more
effective if the language offers in addition:
- separate specification of module interfaces;
- definition of program stubs to be separately
  compiled.

3.2.4 Data Types

Strong typing is requested; data types should
include both enumerated and "range" types.

The motivation for strong typing is its important
implications both for programmer productivity and for
software reliability. However, there must be a controlled
way of overcoming the strong typing restrictions in the few
cases where one needs to.

The gain in clarity obtained by using data types which closely fit the problem is well-known.

Because of the standard word lengths (8-16 bits) of microprocessors, bytes and words can be defined as 8 and 16 bit quantities; there is no need to map these data types onto different word lengths. Among the applications that we have described, real (floating point) numbers are needed for data acquisition and continuous process control applications; they need not be available as a predefined data type of the language, as separate real arithmetic library functions suffice, although of course real data types would be more convenient.

3.2.5 Data Structures

Data structures supported should include arrays, records, and linked data structures. Recursive procedures are not a requirement, but re-entrancy is (so recursion is easy to provide).

Neither arrays with dynamic bounds nor dynamic creation of data structures accessed by a pointer are considered essential because of the rather static data structures found in most industrial applications. Sequential files (as in Pascal) are not useful for real-time systems.

The language should allow initialisation of variables at compile time, and separate allocation of initialised constants, in order to put them into ROM memory.

3.2.6 Assignment and Expressions

The usual arithmetic and relational operators are needed. Assignment of whole aggregates is not required; pointer assignment is sufficient.

3.2.7 Control Structures

Control structures needed are conditional and case statements, and loops with structured jumps. Control structures should be closed; explicit indication of the end of a construct adds to reliability.

3.2.8 Processes, Synchronisation and Communication

It should be possible to define a statically determined number of parallel processes. Each process can be treated as a largely autonomous program. Most forms of high-level process interaction and communication proposed in the literature are acceptable in principle (monitors, rendezvous, mail-boxes, etc.). However, for simplicity, only one of these communication primitives should be present. Moreover, the communication and synchronisation mechanism must be efficiently implemented on a wide variety of architectures ranging from multi-microprocessors with shared memory to truly distributed systems.

The motivation of these requirements is this. For an application system, such as an industrial production line, made of physically identified subsystems, the number of processes is known and fixed. The superiority of high level synchronisation constructs over semaphores has been convincingly argued in the literature (Brinch Hansen 1978); such constructs make programs easier to develop and less error-prone. However the efficiency of high-level communication and synchronisation operations in an industrial environment should be carefully examined. It is possible that the rendezvous technique forces numbers of computational processes to be introduced to improve communication.

Our unwillingness to be categorical about synchronisation and communication primitives stems from the theoretical result that they can always simulate each other and from the pragmatical remark that in this area little sense can be made of comparisons that are not based on experimentation.

The feasibility of structuring systems in this way can be argued as follows. As we can see from the examples of the previous chapter, most application systems use a real-time multi-tasking kernel to define and manage parallel activities (processes or tasks). A concurrent language could be considered as a natural evolution from this approach.

3.2.9 Input-Output

Input-output should be programmed using high-level statements; interrupt handling should be provided.

The motivation for this is that microprocessors are frequently applied to control input-output equipment; it would be uneconomical to impose assembly language for writing extensive parts of the programs. However, it is clear that the large variety of plant peripherals cannot be managed with a predefined set of input-output operations (such as read and write in Pascal). The ability to define procedural interfaces could be a valid solution; there should be a primitive family which can be built on to handle 'odd' devices, and a more convenient-to-use higher level applicable only to conventional devices, e.g. for debugging purposes.

Modula (and other languages) have demonstrated the feasibility of handling input-output devices using high-level statements, given some form of absolute addressing. Interrupts nicely fit into a concurrent language as a specific form of interprocess action.

3.2.10 Exception Handling

A level of treatment of exceptional events should be offered by the language and run-time system.

This is motivated by the frequent need to handle alarms; in some applications some form of fault-tolerance is also required. However when exception handling is not needed, neither the programmer nor the run-time system should incur costs arising from the existence of the features.

Two approaches are possible:

a) Exceptions are viewed as a programming technique, that simplifies abnormal exit from program structures. In this case program development and exception planning take place simultaneously.

b) First the normal functions are designed and
   implemented, then the abnormal actions or
   emergencies are added without affecting the normal
   level.

Little industrial experience exists in this area,
so that it is not possible to choose one of the two
approaches. However, note that exception handling can also
be used for debugging purposes, a case where technique b)
seems preferable.

Exception handling in a multi-process and
distributed environment is a virtually unexplored area,
which presents serious implementation problems.

3.3 REQUIREMENTS FOR THE PROGRAMMING ENVIRONMENT

The conventional host-target approach is assumed;
i.e. application systems are constructed and partially
tested on a host machine rather than directly on the target
hardware.

It is important to distinguish between what host
facilities should be regarded as essential now and what will
be needed in in a few years time. The terms 'near-future
environment' and 'future environment' will be used.
Currently the host environment should concentrate on the
development phase of projects in order to be quickly
realisable, cheap and capable of running on existing limited
host machines. As hardware costs come down, hosts for a
given cost will have greater capability and applications
will become more complex, both enabling and requiring more
facilities in the environment.

3.3.1 Near-future environment

Distribution of the target hardware is the
distinguishing factor compared to existing environments and
is dealt with in some detail in section 3.3.2 below.

The host environment should include at least:

i) A general text editor, for input and modification of program source, documentation, etc.

ii) A file system.

This will be used for storage and retrieval of the software components of an application system, at the various stages of processing, plus other information such as documentation and acceptance test input.

It should be possible to hold different versions of a text. It is desirable to relate each processed component to the relevant version of the relevant program source text(s).

iii) A source language compiler, efficiently implementing separate compilation.

Interface checking between separately-compiled modules is essential to avoid obscure time-consuming errors.

iv) A linker of separately-compiled modules.

It is useful if existing software written in other high-level languages or Assembler can be linked.

v) A program builder.

This will input a description of the target hardware configuration and instructions on the allocation of application system software to the various parts of the hardware, and produce executable code for the target.

Clearly it must allow for a mixture of ROM and RAM memory types. It must also allow for a mixture of hardware types in the target configuration. One method is a object code for a conceptual standard target with an interpreter for each type of processor; this results in slow but compact code. The host itself is normally a 'target' since application systems will be partially tested on the host.

vi) A high-level symbolic debugger.

This will support debugging on the host or on connected target hardware, in terms of the program source text.

vii) A loader for the target.

This might be on-line (e.g. via a communications line) or off-line (e.g. via paper tape or ROM).

Obviously, an on-line loader is preferable. If one is not available it is likely that on-line testing will also not be available.

viii) A good job control language.

This should allow one to receive the completion status reported by called programs and take action on it, as well as facilities for interaction with the user.

Other non-essential tools include:

- a syntax-driven editor;
- a version-management system;
- a target system emulator.

The environment should support multi-user program development for cost-effectiveness and to support multi-programmer projects. The same basic facilities should be available on a range of hosts down to small single-user hosts.

The above tools should be available on different host machines to avoid being tied in to one manufacturer. This means that the interface to the host operating system should be designed to aid portability or that a widely-available (or portable) operating system, such as Unix*, should be used.

The target should provide some elementary debugging facilities in stand-alone mode, to be used after installation of the system or when it is not feasible to test with the target connected to the host.

3.3.2 Target Configuration

A set of compatible boards from a family (such as Intel's Multibus, and TXT's Zeta) defines an architecture. An architecture will often include more than one type of processor. A configuration is a particular arrangement of hardware for a particular application system. The boards of a configuration might belong to a single architecture or a mixture might be used. In most cases the boards will be from a single architecture. In other cases it might be

_____
* UNIX is a trademark of Bell Laboratories.

useful to have boards from another architecture connected by
a serial link (to provide a simple interface).

The ability to configure the target should be
exploited:

- to meet performance and reliability requirements;
- to optimise the cost-effectiveness of the hardware
  system;
- to use the appropriate type of hardware for each
  function of an application system;
- to allow development and testing of the
  application system without needing the full target
  hardware.

These objectives, particularly the last one, mean
that any reference to the configuration should be avoided in
the program source. This means that programs should be
specified at two distinct levels:

- the hardware-independent data structures and
  algorithms;
- the description of the target hardware
  configuration and how the functions of the
  application system are to be allocated to
  different parts of the target.

The separation between these should be complete,
so that no rewriting of the program source is necessary when
the configuration is changed. This has the additional
benefit that some part of the processing of the source code
(e.g. compilation) might also be configuration-independent,
saving resources on rebuilding the program when the
configuration is changed.

It should be noted that dynamic reconfiguration of
the software or hardware is not considered a requirement for
our systems. However we require the capability of aborting,
resetting or restarting object tasks when faults show up.
This is sufficient for the applications we have described.

3.3.3 Future Environments

The scope of the environment should later be extended beyond development to encompass more of the software life cycle. There should be support for the maintenance and upgrading stages of projects and for optional specification and design methodologies. Such future environments will probably appear over the next five years or so.

Maintenance, i.e. correcting errors that become apparent after the application system is installed, will often be done by people other than the developers. This requires information to be held by the environment rather than in programmers' minds. Upgrading, i.e. extending the functions of an application system, requires even more information about the current system, particularly about the requirements, overall assumptions and the specification and design stages. The environment should therefore provide:

- storage of all types of information about the project;
- recording general relationships between items of information; for example, to show how the current system was constructed;
- comprehensive access-rights and binding mechanisms to prevent the inadvertent or unauthorised deletion of information, including relationships.

Conventional filing systems with hierarchical directory structures and simple access-rights mechanisms can only partially achieve these objectives. Thus a 'database' will be needed rather than the filing system of the particular host.

Information about the requirements, specification and design stages should be recorded on the host machine at the very least like documentation. Of course, this is always possible, but users will normally have preferred methods of specifying and/or designing systems and the environment should support these methodologies by specific tools and use of the database facilities to represent the application system at higher levels than the program source text level.

Because future environments will cover the whole
lifetime of application systems (perhaps up to 10 years),
tool portability, database portability and user portability
all will become more important than they are in development
environments of today. Tool and database portability
minimise disruption caused by re-writing and retesting when
a host machine is replaced, and they allow tools developed
for the same environment elsewhere to be easily adopted.
This latter aspect should help to make tools cheaper by
allowing more users to share the cost of developing a tool.
The portability of tools becomes more important as their
number and capability increases with the increased scope of
the environment.

The environment should also provide facilities for
new tools to be composed using existing simpler tools as
well as newly-written software. This technique also helps to
reduce the timescale and cost of tool production.

Portability for human users avoids a learning
phase when the host is replaced or when the user moves to a
different host. To a large extent, tool and database
portability assist user portability, because the user
interface is largely implemented by tools and the database.

Tools that operate by calling other tools can also
be regarded as 'users'. So user portability and tool
portability are aspects of the same objective, which is to
match reduced hardware costs with reduced software
production and user training costs via standardisation.

The environment should include one or more methods
of configuration control, including the semi-automated
construction of application systems from the source text.
This is particularly useful for convenient and correct
rebuilding of a system after changes to it, or for the
construction of a set of closely-related application
systems.

The continuing fall in the cost of hardware will
soon make single-user workstations commonplace. Much of the
environment, especially the database, will still need to be
multi-user to support multi-person projects.

3.4 <u>RUN-TIME ASPECTS</u>

The run-time system provides on any target configuration the support required for loading, executing and debugging object programs.

The following features of the run-time system kernel are required:

i) loading object programs from the host into predefined memory locations of the target;

ii) starting programs;

iii) dynamic memory mangement, if necessary;

iv) handling interrupts and process scheduling on each processor;

v) handling inter-process communication;

vi) interprocessor communication as supported by physical channels of a specific configuration;

vii) exception handling;

ix) handling debugging commands and dialogues with the debugging operator;

The kernel should be organised as separate modules, each to be included only if needed; for example, single-processor configurations need only a simplified run-time system kernel.

The size and performance of the run-time system kernel should be comparable with that of existing multi-tasking real-time kernels for 8 bit machines, such as ZEX and RMX.

Programs may be ROM or RAM resident, a fact that requires different start-up strategies.

As we argued above, multitasking is a requirement, but priorities are not considered an essential feature, because one can always dedicate a processor to a process having high priority requirements; however some form of faster service should be reserved to interrupt routines.

Inter-process communication implements the mechanism present in the language (e.g. rendezvous). Communication between processes allocated to different processors should be transparent to the user; this implies that the run-time system must handle communication

protocols. Other solutions to the problem are discussed
later.

It is sufficient to provide communication between
physically connected processors; a general routing service
is not required.

4

Suitability of Ada and Apse

4.1 <u>INTRODUCTION</u>

In the mid 1970's, the US Department of Defense (DOD) perceived that they could improve both productivity and quality of software production by using fewer and better languages. They embarked on various cycles of identifying requirements, and commissioning competitive designs; this led to the new language, Ada (DOD 1983), which will be the DOD's standard for embedded computer applications. Ada is generally highly regarded and is expected to be very widely used. Organisations like the UK Ministry of Defence (MOD) and Department of Trade and Industry (DTI) and the European Commission are actively supporting its development.

One of the DOD's main stated reasons for language standardisation was that even they could not support several different toolsets; they knew that future software development would require much more support than just a compiler. So, in parallel with the language requirements/design cycle, they started to identify requirements for the Ada software support environment in a series of documents, the last being 'Stoneman' (DOD 1980).

In Stoneman three levels were identified. The kernel ("Kapse") provides the basic facilities needed by software development tools. The "Mapse" (minimal Apse) is the Kapse equipped with a minimal toolset to support Ada. An "Apse" (Ada Programming Support Environment) is the Mapse augmented by a richer toolset to support the whole software life cycle and perhaps other languages.

Although Ada was designed in response to a call for a language for embedded computer systems in defence

applications, the language covers a larger application area.
Industrial application systems (such as those discussed in
Chapter 2) are embedded systems like those Ada is designed
to cover. Compared with defence systems, these applications
are generally more conservative, and do not require all
features of Ada. In this respect, our industrial
applications allow for significant simplifications in a
language that has been widely criticised for being too large
and complicated. On the other hand, the industrial systems
we are considering include distributed computer
implementations, whereas no specific attention has been paid
to distributed programming in the design of Ada or to the
support of multimicroprocessor targets in Apse design.

The aim of this chapter is to evaluate Ada and
Apse with respect to the intended industrial applications,
and to distributed computer implementations.

It must be emphasised again that this discussion
is with respect to the type of applications we have
illustrated in Chapter 2. These applications are relatively
"small", and in some ways undemanding, as compared to the
wide range of applications for which Ada is designed, so it
would be surprising if Ada did not exceed our requirements
in many ways.

In section 4.2, each main feature of the language
is discussed in relation to the language requirements
outlined in Chapter 3, and qualified by one of the
following:

-   exceeds requirements
-   meets requirements
-   inadvisable feature
-   below requirements

In section 4.3, the suitability of Apses for the
intended applications is discussed with reference to the
current state of Ada/Apse projects.

In section 4.4, the implicit target dependencies
that might be present in an Ada source program are discussed
to show the obstacles Ada and Apse meet when supporting
distributed target systems.

4.2 SUITABILITY OF ADA LANGUAGE CONCEPTS FOR THE INTENDED APPLICATIONS

This section considers those aspects of our identified requirements which do not relate specifically to distributed systems. The requirements of distributed systems will be considered later.

4.2.1 Program structure and program development

Ada offers the user an integrated approach to specification and separate compilation of program units which allows effective checking of interfaces by the compiler [meets requirements], as well as language-level support of program methodology, both top-down by stubs, and bottom-up by package and task specifications [meets requirements].

Ada provides four structural units in which declarations can occur: blocks, subprograms, packages and tasks. Packages and tasks have separate specifications and bodies (but for subprograms this separation is optional). This characteristic is highly desirable, both to separate function from method of implementation of subprograms and packages, and to allow reliable construction of large programs by many programmers, especially during the initial requirements specification; we were tempted to say that this is not essential for small industrial application projects, but it forces a good design methodology and it might be very useful for those applications in which an initial general specification is made more precise as the project proceeds [meets requirements].

Each Ada structural unit can appear inside any of the other units, and this nesting can in principle go on indefinitely, with only the restriction that a block, being a statement, cannot appear in a package specification. Multi-level nesting of structural units can also be used effectively to hide inner details and for protection, but this feature is not considered essential for industrial automation projects. Information hiding can be achieved without nesting by using a separately-compiled library

package: in this case visibility and lifetime are separated,
unlike nesting. Moreover, in practice, some nesting
combinations will arise rarely (as, in a static environment,
tasks will always be inside packages or the main subprogram,
not inside other tasks or subprograms; blocks will only
occasionally occur inside other blocks, etc.)[exceeds
requirements].

4.2.2 Data Types

"A type is characterised by a set of values and a
set of operations" (Ada Language Reference Manual ("LRM"),
section 3.3). In Ada every type declaration introduces a new
type distinct from any other type. This is the fundamental
rule of strong typing, which means that the types of all
data objects in the program are checked for consistency with
their usage. This is a useful aid to the rapid development
of correct programs, since it ensures that many errors are
detected at compilation time [meets requirements].

Real numbers

Real (floating and fixed point) numbers need not
be available as a predefined data type, as in Ada. A
separate real arithmetic library is probably enough [exceeds
requirements].

Subtypes

Subtypes are just subsets of other types known as
base types. The subset is defined by a constraint; it may be
the complete set, but there is no way of restricting the set
of operations of the base type. We see the value of
subtypes for security but it has considerable run-time cost,
which is increased by the fact that exceptions impede
compile-time flow analysis. If the checking of constraint
errors were optional, subtypes would be a desirable feature
[exceeds requirements].

Derived types

New types derived from an existing type (parent
type) inherit certain characteristics from the parent type.
Derived types enable the programmer to have the protection
of strong typing but also to convert type explicitly where

required. The cost of derived types does not seem excessive
[meets requirements].

Representation specifications

These are of different kinds. They are necessary
for connecting interrupts to task entry points, for
assigning specific addresses to data and code, for linking
together modules written in different languages or for
different microprocessors [meets requirements].

However, the complex provision for controlling the
physical representation of structured objects seems
unnecessary unless records or arrays can be shared by
different processors [exceeds requirements].

4.2.3 Data Structures

Ada provides for:

Arrays

of one, two or more dimensions [meets
requirements].

Arrays with dynamic bounds (unconstrained) are not
considered essential because of the usually static data
structures found in most our industrial applications
[exceeds requirements]. Selecting contiguous sections of a
one-dimensional array (slicing) exceeds requirements.

Records

[meets requirements]

Discriminated record types

Here some of the record components are known as
discriminants, and the remaining components can depend upon
these; this can be useful (but not necessary) for managing
storage and saving space [exceeds requirements].

Access types

These are for allocating new objects whose
lifetime is independent of block structure. This feature,
for its dynamic characteristic, is not considered essential
for industrial applications, in which the number of
processes to control and of variables to manipulate is
generally a well determined constant [exceeds
requirements]. (In Ironman it is stated that these features

"are intended primarily for support portions of embedded
computer software".)

Ada lacks a static pointer type for accessing a
variable indirectly. The lack of a way to declare static
pointers in data structures limits what can be put in ROM
rather than on the heap (in RAM). Access objects are
elegant but not as useful as traditional pointers [below
requirements].

Constant and variable initialisation

This is an essential feature [meets requirements];
default values specification for record components in type
declarations probably exceeds requirements.

4.2.4 Assignment, Expressions and Control Structures

In these areas, the Ada language generally meets
requirements. The following features however exceed
requirements:
- short-circuit logical operators
- exponentiation
- qualified expressions
- static expressions
- literal expressions

4.2.5 Program Units

Ada allows three forms of program units from which
programs can be composed:

(i) Subprograms

An executable program unit is invoked by a
subprogram call; the unit may be a procedure or a function.
The specification of a procedure specifies its identifier,
and its formal parameters if any; the specification of a
function specifies its designator, its formal parameters if
any, and the subtype of the returned value [meets
requirements]. Parameters may be positional or named
[exceeds requirements], and, if a program declaration
specifies a default value for an 'in' parameter, then the
corresponding parameter may be omitted from a call. This

exceeds requirements even if default parameters might be
useful for library routines. The semantics of parameter
passing for non scalar objects is not defined in Ada; this
causes some uncertainty about the effects of subprogram
executions in the presence of exceptions.

In Ada there can be several subprograms with the
same name distinguished by the properties of their
parameters. Using the same name for distinct meanings in the
same context is called overloading; it is a useful feature
to implement, for example, I/O operations, but it is not
considered essential [exceeds requirements]. Recursion is
not required, since its major use is for compiler writing,
but reentrancy is, which will probably give recursion as a
bonus.

(ii) Packages

These allow the specification of logically related
entities. In their simplest form, packages can represent
pools of common data and type declarations [meets
requirements]. More generally, packages can be used to
describe groups of related entities, whose inner workings
are protected and concealed from their users.

(iii) Tasks

These will be discussed in section 4.2.8.

(iv) Generics

The generic mechanism allows the programmer to
parameterise subprograms and packages and to create several
instances of an abstract object differing from each other in
the values of the generic parameters (types or subprograms
or values). In this way it is not necessary to repeat a
piece of program for all the different types to which we
might wish it to apply, if its logic is independent of the
types. Our needs are often restricted to changes in address
or data structure dimension and we rarely need to be
parametric with regard to more general data structures, so

that conditional compilation would probably be sufficient
for our problems [exceeds requirements].

4.2.6 Input Output

Real-time systems require a programming language
that allows the programmer to decide the policy of resource
management, that gives good visibility of I/O processes, and
an efficient synchronisation mechanism with the external
environment. "Virtual devices" or "files", used for example
in Concurrent Pascal, introduce a virtualisation level and
fit the standard devices well, but are not very useful for
dedicated devices, such as process control peripherals and
graphic devices. Moreover this approach requires powerful
and large runtime support which must be updated for every
new device attached to the system.

On the other hand, Ada does not have any intrinsic
feature for input/output but relies on special packages
[meets requirements], and encourages the use of package and
task features for implementing I/O facilities. The aim of
this style of programming in Ada is to keep the machine
dependency (tied in with I/O management) in as limited a
context as possible [meets requirements].

The LRM proposes some standard packages for common
I/O facilities (SEQUENTIAL_IO and DIRECT_IO for general
handling of files, and TEXT_IO for handling streams of
characters), and for low level I/O operations
(LOW_LEVEL_IO), but it is easy to develop different I/O
packages for different application areas without affecting
the language itself [meets requirements]. The overloading
mechanism is a useful instrument for attaining this aim.

Ada interrupt facilities allow efficient
synchronisation of software with hardware [meets
requirements].

4.2.7 Exceptions

Ada provides a dynamic mechanism for unusual termination which allows exit from program units bypassing the normal termination mechanism.

Exceptions may be defined by the user or predefined by the system [meets requirements].

In our applications, where erroneous situations must be quickly dealt with, to achieve some degree of fault-tolerance, exception handling is really useful [meets requirements].

However it seems sufficient to handle exceptions only at the outermost level of packages and tasks to perform recovery actions. Therefore exception propagation exceeds our requirements. (This feature of Ada has also been considered inadvisable by Hoare (1981).) Overloading of exception names exceeds requirements.

4.2.8 Tasks

Ada provides facilities for tasks to be created and terminated or aborted as the program executes, as well as tasks which have effectively infinite lifetime.

To achieve infinite lifetime each task must be declared in the specification of a library package or in the outermost declarative part of the body of a library package or the main subprogram. Library packages are those library units which are referenced by the main subprogram in its with clause(s). They are elaborated, with any tasks activated, before entry into the main subprogram [meets requirements].

For the application area described in Chapter 2, there is no requirement for dynamically-created tasks [exceeds requirements]. A pre-determined number of tasks, each with infinite lifetime, is quite sufficient for the intended industrial applications even if dynamic task creation can allow for more elegant solutions to certain classes of problems (e.g. the recovery from processor or software failures and the implementation of communications between loosely connected processors).

Ada treats tasks in many respects as low level entities like data objects. Ada allows task types, task access types, task objects and task access objects. A task could be created as part of evaluating an expression in an executable statement [exceeds requirements]. However, the conventional approach to application system design would treat tasks at a much higher level, being design concepts whereas the use of data objects is just a detail of implementation. The Ada approach recognises that parallel processing is often needed (or can be used to advantage) at detailed levels of design as well as at the highest level. However, for the intended application area this 'low level' tasking represented by task objects is not essential [exceeds requirements].

As regards task access objects, there are two principal reasons why they might be used in an application system:

a) to allow mutual calling between tasks where one of the tasks must be written without knowledge of the other, such as a server task controlling some resource used by several user tasks.

In Ada the server task does not automatically know the identity of the calling user. To overcome this the user can pass its identity to the server in the form of a task access object. The users must be of the same type and the user task must have been created by an allocator in an assignment to a task access object in the main code (or parent task). The user identity has to be explicitly passed to the task by a call to one of its entries.

b) to allow the connection of tasks to be determined at run-time.

This has two benefits. Firstly, it avoids the compile-time binding caused by using the names of task objects in the declaration of task types; this also means that all tasks of the type can call the referenced tasks. Secondly, if an entry call is made using a task access object instead of a task object, the identity of the called task can be changed at run-time, by assignment to the task

access object. Amongst other things, this can be useful for
fault-tolerant systems.

Since with a static set of tasks the identities of
all tasks are (or could be) known at the time the source
text is written, the use of task access objects for both
reasons could be avoided [exceeds requirements]. This would
require the use of conditional statements to select between
specific tasks on each entry call. But this is inefficient
at run-time compared to a single assignment to a task access
object. It also spreads the knowledge of the set of tasks
throughout the program.

Ada allows two forms of interaction between tasks,
which respectively reflect the shared-memory and local
environment models:

- communication by shared variables;
- communication and synchronisation by procedure
  call.

Communication by shared non-local variables may
present problems because it presupposes a shared-memory
hardware implementation, and because careful synchronisation
is required to avoid access conflicts among the tasks which
share a variable. In some applications shared variables
must be used because of their efficiency. However some form
of protection in accessing shared variables should be
available. In Ada, communication by shared variables is
unprotected [inadvisable feature].

The mechanism for communication and
synchronisation between tasks by procedure call in Ada is
the rendezvous, which is realised with entry calls (in the
calling task) and accept statements (in the called task).
Entry calls and accept statements provide a high level
mechanism which is convenient to use, even if there will be
cases when low level primitives are more appropriate [meets
requirements].

The conditional entry mechanism by which an entry
call takes place only if it can be "immediately" accepted by
the called task is a rather unsafe concept in a distributed
environment where routing-message delays may effect response

time (see also section 4.4) [inadvisable feature].

Ada provides a way to specify task priorities by pragma. In addition interrupt handlers are viewed as tasks with a priority exceeding any other task, thus creating a two level priority system.

Higher priority for interrupt handling meets requirements, whereas the possibility of assigning explicit priorities to tasks is important only when a system tends to have a high degree of multi-tasking for each processor: a case that multi-microprocessor organisations tend to avoid [exceeds requirements].

The method of passing parameters in a task rendezvous is defined to be as for subprogram calls. For scalar objects this is by copy but for record and array types the construction system can choose between call by copy or call by reference. This choice has no effect on the outcome of a rendezvous unless data is shared between tasks or an unhandled exception occurs during the rendezvous [inadvisable feature].

Passing parameters by reference can only practically be used if tasks share memory. Similarly access objects, which are explicit references, can be parameters only in this case. Further, the memory containing the object referenced by the access object must be addressable by the called task.

4.3 SUITABILITY OF APSE FACILITIES

4.3.1 Background

Apses are being designed to meet more sophisticated requirements than those placed on existing software support environments (SSE's).

Most present day operating systems are designed more for running software than for developing it. Few software tools are provided as standard. Today's most highly respected SSE is Unix, which started as a single user system some ten years ago. Many excellent software tools are available under Unix and they can interface to each other through the pipe mechanism. Nevertheless, they are often difficult to use in combination and present differing interfaces to the user. Apses are designed as integrated environments to meet specific requirements such as:

(i) Support for all stages of the software life cycle.

Existing environments concentrate on the development phase. Future SSE's should support the whole cycle, from requirements specification, through design and development, to maintenance.

(ii) Support for all roles in the project team.

Managers and clerical staff, as well as programmers.

(iii) Configuration control.

Understanding and managing modules of software, the relationships between them, and the way in which they are configured in systems, is an important problem. Effective solutions make substantial demands on the SSE.

(iv) Integration and user-friendliness.

The SSE and the tools within it must be easy to use. The tools must therefore be well integrated, i.e. they must be based on a common set of concepts, present similar interfaces to the user and interface well with each other.

(v) Host/target support.

The growing importance of embedded systems and microprocessors and the demands made by the SSE's themselves, both point to more frequent separation of the host (used for development) and the target (which runs the system being developed). Even when the host and target are identical, it is helpful to separate them conceptually.

(vi) Portability.

It is important that the SSE looks the same from machine to machine ("user portability"); that support for a system being developed can be moved from host to host ("project portability"); and that the SSE itself and its target specific components can be adapted cheaply to new hosts and new targets.

A crucial consequence of the above requirements is the replacement of the conventional "filing system" by a much more powerful "database".

The requirements above, notably the first three, can only be met by making available, to users and to tools, a great deal of information about the relationships between modules.

The first phase of Apse design and implementation has seen four major efforts:

- Ada Language System (ALS) (Softech, for the US Army) (Softech 1982).

This is a limited Unix like system. It started in 1980 and first deliveries, for a Vax host, have already been made.

- Ada Integrated Environment (AIE) (Intermetrics, for the USAF) (Intermetrics 1982).

This is a much more sophisticated system, with a novel and powerful database. Intermetrics was selected after a competitive design phase in 1980/1. Implementation, for an IBM host, has started.

- UK Apse (Mchapse) (SPL et al. 1981).

This design was started in 1980 by a consortium of SPL, SDL, SSL and ICL. Implementation work has now started. The UK Apse has been funded by the UK DTI, MOD and others. It has a sophisticated database, using an entity-relationship-attribute model, not like the Intermetrics approach.

- Portable Ada Programming System (PAPS) (Olivetti, DDC and Christian Rovsing, part funded by the European Commission) (Olivetti 1982).

Design started in 1981; it should be running in 1984 on an Olivetti mini. In their early stages, Olivetti and the UK team exchanged ideas. There is a substantial database similar to that of the UK Apse.

There are several other projects to develop Ada compilers, in Universities (e.g. York UK, New York, Karlsruhe) and by manufacturers (e.g. Rolm, Digital).

Each of the above Apse implementations will initially be a minimal Apse containing a relatively small toolset running on a basic Kapse. The toolset is designed to

meet initial requirements, i.e. the development of Ada
programs for relatively easy targets.

All of these Apses will easily meet the
requirements of Chapter 2 with the exception of building
programs for distributed targets. They are completely usable
in themselves but will grow as time passes by the addition
of tools. They incorporate features to support such
extension, principally a powerful database (in the Kapse).

The Kapses are only partly host-independent, while
the rest of the Apses should be largely host and target
independent.

These Apses have a number of relevant factors in
common:

1) They support the full Ada language.
2) The published work only covers the higher
   functional levels of Apses rather than the more
   detailed design where assumptions preventing
   applicability to distributed systems might appear.
3) The problems of implementing Ada on distributed
   targets do not appear to have been addressed yet.

Overcoming any inadequacy of the language in
respect of distributed systems will require action in any
Apse. One reason for the low priority of distributed
targets is that minimising the cost and difficulty of adding
a new type of target to the range that can be supported is
an important objective of any Apse. Thus work so far has
concentrated on the target-independent parts of the Apse.

4.3.2 Recent Developments

At the time of writing, there have been numerous
developments on the Apse scene. No doubt this section will
be out of date when it appears.

Both the UK Apse and the Intermetrics AIE seem to
have run into funding difficulties. In each case the
compiler work is continuing while the environment work is
reassessed in the light of their respective funding
problems.

Other important initiatives are underway:
- There is a major programme (SPERBER) in Germany to develop an Apse.
- The DOD, concerned at the proliferation of Apses, have started an initiative to define a Common Apse Interface Set (CAIS).

CAIS is intended as an interface which could be implemented on top of existing environments, such as ALS and AIE, or could be implemented directly. It would thus contribute to tool portability between Apses, and might well develop into a standard Kapse for the future.

Early drafts of CAIS have been published (DOD 1984). It is hoped to have a Version 1 Standard in early 1985, and a second version in 1987.

- There are also various projects to define SSE's to meet the general requirements outlined above, but to support several languages, not just Ada.

Notable amongst these is the Portable Common Tool Environment (PCTE) being defined within the European Commission's Esprit programme; PAPS has been an important source for PCTE.

It is noteworthy that both CAIS and PCTE have also adopted an entity-relationship-attribute approach to their databases.

4.3.3 The Mapse Designs

We will describe the relevant parts of the UK Apse design, to which we are closest, to illustrate the contexts in which support for distributed targets must be implemented. Most Apses are very similar in these respects.

The UK Apse

Keeping the cost of re-targeting down is an important factor in Apse design. Obviously the conventional target-independent front-end and target-dependent back-end Ada compiler structure is used, but also the linker is target-independent. It concentrates on handling the Ada aspects of the program that cannot be dealt with by the compiler (because it only sees parts of the complete program

in any one submission). The output of the linker is
processed by a target-dependent builder which produces a
suitable representation of the program. Because of the
diversity of possible target architectures no work has yet
been done on the builder except to note general aspects that
must be handled by every builder, such as expression-
evaluation. (So even the builder has a target-independent
part.)

Similarly the symbolic debugger is insulated from
any details of the target by a standard 'Monitored Context'
interface to the executing program, implemented for each
target.

The output of the Ada compiler is stored in a
'domain' structure which implements the Ada 'library file'.
The target for each domain is specified when the domain is
created. This information is used to select the appropriate
target-dependent parts of the construction system
automatically.

So the UK Apse attempts to maximise the target-
independent parts of program construction. It contains no
facilities specifically for distributed targets, but of
course the compiler back-end, program builder, Monitored
Context interface and Ada run-time system will be provided
for each type of target. The question is thus whether any
assumptions that are not true for distributed systems have
been made in deciding what is target-independent.

The Ada compiler is implemented as a set of sub-
tools controlled by a 'compiler-manager' tool. Thus it can
be taken apart and the sub-tools used separately. In
particular the front-end and back-end can be separated.
Front-end output can be stored in the domain. Whether the
sources of these compiler subtools will be available or only
their executable forms depends on the commercial licensing
conditions.

The Ada linker operates on back-end output. This
means that a link which could be done once only on front-end
output must be done one for each different form of back-end
output from the Ada source. There is a partial-link ability

which imposes no restriction on the set of compilation units
to be linked. Thus the code of a task type can be linked,
putting together the sub-units of the body and any library
package or subprogram code which is to be replicated.

The compilation and linking system includes a
'section' concept which can be used to keep the code of task
types and shared library package or subprogram code
logically separate in the single input to the builder.

The domain has no provision for storing several
different forms of back-end output for a given compilation
unit (or partial-link). This is necessary for code which has
multiple copies running on different processor types. A
versioning system for the domain which would allow this is
an extension to the design of the domain which has been
considered and deferred. (A program must be linked out of
one domain to avoid the need for the linker to repeat the
checking already done by the compiler.)

The Monitored Context interface for debugging is
unsatisfactory in one respect. It assumes there is only one
copy of the code for a task type or library package or
subprogram. It needs to be modified to include the name of
the task object on any reference to a code address.

The Olivetti Apse (PAPS)

The functional specifications of the tools of the
PAPS are very similar to those in the UK Apse. Thus the
comments in 4.3.1 about the UK Apse almost all also apply to
the PAPS. There are minor differences. One which has
relevance is that partial-linking is restricted to operate
only on sub-trees of sub-units. Thus the sub-units of the
body of a task type can be linked but any replicated library
package or subprogram code cannot be included.

The USAF Apse (Intermetrics)

At the level of functionality considered in this
document the relevant aspects of this Apse are much the same
as for the two Apses already considered. One difference is
a facility for alternative versions of body units in the
compilation domain; this will be useful for generating
directly-executable code with more than one type of

processor in a target.

4.4 SUITABILITY OF ADA/APSE FOR DISTRIBUTED TARGETS

There are in Ada inherent target dependencies
concerning the assumption of a single address space, which
impede the use of Ada as a programming language for
distributed applications. These target dependencies and
their relation to the construction system are the subject of
this section, whereas strategies for developing distributed
programs in Ada will be discussed in Chapters 5 and 6.

A program written in Ada might have target
dependence for the following reasons:

- non-rendezvous forms of inter-task communication,
  via data in library packages and via nested task
  type declarations;
- the assumption that there is a centralised heap;
- the conditional entry call facility;
- the use of access objects in rendezvous;
- the definition of packages STANDARD and SYSTEM;
- assumptions in the representation clauses
  concerned with the target hardware.

These are discussed in sections 4.4.1 to 4.4.6
respectively.

The design of Ada inter-task communication was
probably influenced by an assumption that is not true for
distributed hardware, but this is not serious. Section 4.4.7
discusses this point.

4.4.1 Intertask communication

The primary difficulty in mapping Ada onto a
distributed target is that communication between Ada tasks
is not restricted solely to the task rendezvous. The
library package mechanism allows independent tasks to share
static data structures, (declared in the specification of a
library package or in the outermost declarative part of the
package body). These structures can contain heap objects
(i.e. access objects), set up by library package
initialisation code. The facility to nest task type

declarations extends this data-sharing ability to include
objects on the stacks of ancestor tasks.

Both the library package mechanism and the nesting
mechanism also allow tasks to share code.

These library package and nesting mechanisms for
inter-task communication probably derive from an assumption
that the target has a single memory. It is difficult to
support them when the shared code and data are not directly
addressable by all the processors executing the tasks.

Of course direct access to shared data may be
needed for performance, where the overhead of a server task
to handle access to the data would not be acceptable.
Nested task types are also valuable, to arrange the
inheritance of the parent task's context with little run-
time overhead. Thus these Ada facilities cannot simply be
banned.

4.4.2 The heap

There is an assumption in the underlying hardware
model of Ada that there is only one central heap. (For
example, the use of a length clause to specify the
collection size for an access type, discussed below in
4.4.6.) In reality, the heap will normally be partitioned
when the target is distributed.

4.4.3 Entry Calls and Conditional Entry Calls

Consider the following Ada select statement in a
called task T:

```
        select
            when CONDITION_1 =>
                accept ENTRY_1 do ... end;
        or
            when CONDITION_2 =>
                accept ENTRY_2 do ... end;
        end select;
```

Ada states that the selection of one of such open
alternatives occurs immediately if a corresponding
rendezvous is possible. (If several alternatives can be

selected, an arbitrary one of them is selected.)

These semantics are clear only in a shared memory
system; in a distributed system, "immediately" is a concept
that requires some caution. To state that a task S is ready
to establish a rendezvous with T, suitable messages must be
exchanged between S and T, which cannot be performed
"immediately".

The conditional entry call facility of Ada is
intended for use by tasks that cannot afford to be
substantially delayed waiting for rendezvous. (Effectively
it is an entry call with zero timeout.) The assumption is
that the run-time system can quickly establish if the called
task is ready to accept the call or not. This is not in
general true for a distributed target; there could be
significant delay in the data transmission involved in
querying another part of the run-time system (e.g.
contention for a channel, communications failure).

Thus the user must be careful in the use of this
facility. Where necessary, the user should deploy a
subsidiary buffer task to absorb any entry call delay, with
the main task making a conditional entry call on the buffer
task. However there seems no reason to ban the facility.

It would be desirable for the construction system
to allow the user to declare that the conditional call
facility is used between a pair of tasks. The construction
system could then report circumstances where the
communication between the relevant parts of the run-time
system might be unacceptably slow.

In addition to the conditional entry call
facility, the entry call with timeout facility and the
selective wait facility both assume that communication
between parts of the run-time system is fast, since the
timeouts are cancelled when the rendezvous is started rather
than when it is completed. However this is not serious
since in practice generous timeouts will be used, to detect
failure of part of the system rather than to cope with mere
delays in communication.

4.4.4 Access objects as rendezvous parameters

Clearly there must be a restriction on the access objects that can be passed on rendezvous since such objects are explicit references to data structures in memories that might not be addressable by the processor executing the called task. In certain cases copying of the access object and associated objects into a heap partition local to the called task would be consistent with the intention of the user, but this would not generally be true. Often access objects will be pointers internal to a data structure (e.g. a linked list) and operations are intended to occur on the single data structure. Copy semantics would be totally inappropriate.

Therefore if an access object (or a composite object involving one or more access objects) is a parameter in a rendezvous the processors of the calling and called tasks must both be able to address the memory containing the physical heap partition for the access type.

4.4.5 Packages STANDARD and SYSTEM and related pragmas

The application system is a single Ada program. Package STANDARD is the predefined context of every compilation unit. It is not explicitly mentioned in a with clause. Package SYSTEM is also predefined and defines various details of the target hardware, and does have to be referenced in a with clause if used.

The single-memory homogeneous hardware model of Ada is reflected in these packages.

There is only one package STANDARD, which defines types INTEGER and FLOAT. However the generation of efficient code requires that the lengths of the values of these types should be lengths directly supported by the processor instruction set. Thus there is an assumption that processors are of one type only.

There is only one package SYSTEM and it defines:

- a single type ADDRESS (thus assuming a single type of processor-MMU combination);
- a single length in bits of a STORAGE_UNIT (thus assuming a single type of memory);
- a single MEMORY_SIZE (thus assuming one memory).

Similarly the definitions of the maximum and minimum integers and so on assume a single type of memory, a single type of floating-point unit and so on.

Related pragmas SYSTEM_NAME, STORAGE_UNIT and MEMORY_SIZE re-define the entities of the same name in package SYSTEM. It might be expected that these pragmas would be designed to allow local definition of these values for the compilation unit in which they appear. However the use of any of these pragmas causes the implicit recompilation of package SYSTEM and deletion of any compilation units dependent on SYSTEM. So these pragmas implement a special mechanism to provide controlled modification of the pre-defined package SYSTEM, rather than a mechanism for coping with non-homogeneous hardware.

4.4.6 Target-dependent representation clauses and attributes

The representation clauses that reflect the target hardware fall into five categories:

 (i) connection of interrupt locations to task entries;
 (ii) locating code or data at specific addresses;
 (iii) specifying the internal representation of data objects of user-defined types (e.g. length in bits of simple objects, packing the components of composite objects);
 (iv) specifying a limit to the amount of heap that can be used for objects of a given access type;
 (v) allocating a number of storage units for the activation of a given task (or objects of a given task type).

The first two of these reflect the knowledge of physical devices that must be incorporated into the Ada source of I/O drivers. This is unavoidable. However the

compiler should preserve the information in these
representation clauses for later checking of allocation
constraints. Of course, interrupt locations must include
the number of the processor, and addresses for code or data
must include memory indication.

If the representation clauses of type (iii) are
used for efficient mapping of data objects of user-defined
types onto memory the user must accept the target dependence
thereby built into the Ada source.

Representation clauses of type (iv) reflect the
single-memory hardware model since they do not give adequate
control over a distributed heap. In practice their meaning
will be different: the overall limit becomes a limit applied
to each partition of a distributed heap. This interpretation
is not entirely satisfactory but could be useful. Indeed
there should not be any mechanism requiring control of the
total allocation in all parts of a distributed heap.

The use of representation clauses of type (v) will
add target dependence, since stack sizes and so on are
dependent on the type of processor executing the task. For
example for processors implementing a procedure-call
instruction the space needed to save the current context on
entry to procedures will depend on the type of processor.
However this form of dependence is not serious because task
activation sizes will only need to be accurately calculated
for production versions of the application system.

The use of representation clauses in the Ada
source to give instructions about particular data types
cannot be replaced by some external form of specification
(which could easily be changed without affecting the basic
Ada source) because of the scoping of types.

There are various pre-defined attributes that
relate to the hardware:

(i) STORAGE_SIZE for an access type, giving the amount
    of heap space reserved for objects of this type.
    This will be interpreted like the STORAGE_SIZE
    representation clause to refer only to the local
    part of the heap.

(ii) STORAGE_SIZE for a task type, giving the
activation size. See the discussion of the
representation clause above.

(iii) Various attributes relating to aspects of the
floating-point hardware (MACHINE_EMAX and so on).
These should be interpreted correctly, referring
to the type of processor for which the compilation
unit is compiled.

(iv) ADDRESS for an object. Again this should be
interpreted correctly, referring to the type of
processor-MMU combination that will execute the
task of which this compilation unit is part.

Whilst on this subject it should be noted that
there might be a need to add attributes for distributed
targets to those in the current Ada definition. (Such
implementation-dependent attributes are allowed in LRM
4.1.4.) For example an attribute giving the identity of the
processor running a a task could be useful. Another useful
facility could be a pragma to contain information to be
preserved by the compiler to be passed on to later
construction system tools. The compiler would not analyse
the contents of such pragmas.

4.4.7 Ada inter-task communication

The basic method provided by Ada is the
synchronous rendezvous. No form of asynchronous
communication, such as message-passing, is provided.
(Instead it must be built on top of the synchronous
rendezvous.) One reason for this is to avoid an arbitrary
amount of buffering space in the run-time system. By not
providing asynchronous communication Ada avoids deadlocks
caused by exhaustion of run-time system buffer space.

If the called task is not ready to rendezvous the
calling task is suspended. The run-time system can
therefore use the data space of the calling task to hold
information until the rendezvous can proceed. This assumes
that the run-time system for the called task can freely
access this information. This is not in general true for a

distributed target.

The intended approach could still be used, but at the cost of inter-processor communication for access to the calling task's data space. It will often be preferable for the run-time system of the called task to buffer information rather than request another transmission when the rendezvous is ready to proceed.

Thus in practice the run-time system might need to provide buffering for an arbitrary number of calling tasks. This is not a serious problem, since executives that provide asynchronous communication cope with it, but it is a departure from the intention of the language designers.

4.5 CONCLUSIONS

Ada meets or exceeds most requirements, with two noteworthy exceptions: static pointers and distributed computation. The second of these has been discussed in detail in section 4.4.

As Ironman (DOD 1978) states, Ada "should be as small as possible consistent with the needs of the intended applications". For the applications we have studied, Ada exceeds our requirements in many ways.

Ada consistently provides more than we require, by offering individually appealing, well conceived concepts which together make up a language of complexity far exceeding currently used languages for microprocessors. There is obvious concern for the impact of this on the following:

- size and cost of host environment;
- size and performance of target environment;
- training of personnel.

We expect that increased hardware cost effectiveness will soon offset the first two difficulties. The last one is probably the most important, since it does not seem to be an easy and quick process to teach Ada to programmers who are currently reluctant to quit assembly language programming for PL/M or Pascal. On the other hand,

our experience of the ease of teaching Ada to students who
already know Pascal is very encouraging.

All the Apses we have studied could form sensible
environments within which to implement tools to support
distributed targets. However, none of the designs have yet
given any consideration to the specific problems of
distributed targets.

5
Strategies for developing distributed systems

5.1 CHARACTERISTICS OF DISTRIBUTED SYSTEMS

From the discussion of requirements for distributed computing systems, we can summarise the characteristics of such systems:

1) A distributed system is composed of nodes connected by communications links;

2) each node consists of one or more processors with memory which might be private or might be shared between some or all processors. The nodes may be heterogeneous (e.g. they may contain different processors), and may provide different computing capabilities; usually however they belong to the same computer family (e.g. Intel, or Zilog);

3) no assumption is made about communication links, but as a special case nodes may be connected through local communication networks (such as Ethernet);

4) on each node resides one or more functional software components; some of these must be allocated to a specific node because they are strictly related to physical I/O devices; the others may be allocated to any node either under explicit control of the programmer (to meet specific application requirements) or automatically by the system;

5) functional components residing on different nodes interact for the purpose of performing some system-wide functions.

5.2 DESIRABLE STAGES OF DESIGN AND DEVELOPMENT

The desirable approach to the design and development of distributed computing software can be summarised in the following phases:

1) identify functional components and the overall structure of the software system according to the functional requirements of the application;
2) correct the distributed program as far as possible;
3) describe the target system configuration;
4) allocate software allocation units to physical nodes according to the physical requirements of the application.

Phases 1 and 2 must be as far as possible independent of the target configuration and the specific allocation, to allow repeated execution of phases 3 and 4 without changing the software definition (an important goal during the prototyping of the system and for later evolution).

Ada does not provide any means for defining distributed software, like every other language not specifically intended for distributed programming. In particular Ada itself does not allow phases 3 and 4 to be expressed. Potentially, these phases could be realised by adding special tools to existing Apse systems; i.e. distribution is imposed on the program, rather than included in it.

5.3 APPROACHES TO BE CONSIDERED

What approach should one take to using Ada to write a system for a distributed target? We need to consider the feasibility and desirability of each of the following possibilities:

A. "Full Ada, one program". Use full Ada to write the system as a single Ada program. Since Ada has no facilities to express the distributed nature of the target, and the user is not being restricted,

this option implies that the system is being
designed without consideration of the possible
distribution of the target.

B. "Full Ada, multiple programs". Use full Ada to
write the system as multiple Ada programs. Here
the splitting into programs, and the nature of the
interfaces between them, are decided by the user,
presumably taking into account the nature of
likely target configurations.

C. "Uniformly-restricted Ada". Write the system as a
single Ada program, accepting restrictions on the
use of Ada throughout the system, so as to make
distribution of the system possible, but without
influencing the design by consideration of the
nature of likely target configurations.

D. "Non-uniform restriction of Ada". Write the
system as a single Ada program, accepting
restrictions on the use of Ada at the interfaces
where the system may be split for the separate
parts of the distributed system. The system will
be designed with possible distribution in mind,
but without absolute binding to a specific target
configuration.

At first sight, option A might be considered the
most desirable, especially in view of the need to avoid
overtones of "subset" Ada. We do not recommend it, because
of difficulties arising out of the nature of Ada.

These difficulties are serious. The next section
analyses them in some depth, so that the deficiencies of
option A are fully appreciated before we return to the
discussion of the other approaches.

5.4 THE PRINCIPAL PROBLEMS OF USING FULL ADA; SHARED CODE AND DATA

The term 'shared' is used to refer to code and
data that can be accessed directly by more than one task by
use of its Ada identifier rather than only via a task

rendezvous. Sharing can arise via the two main visibility
mechanisms of Ada:

- Nesting. A task type declaration nested in an
  enclosing structure automatically has visibility
  of some of the structure's code and data.
- Several task objects using the same library
  package. This means that the body of the type
  declaration of each task object refers to code
  and/or data in the visible part of the
  specification of the library package.

In both cases it is the task type declarations
that are relevant rather than the declarations of the task
objects.

(i) Shared data
  The sharing of data causes at least six apparent
problems:

- Because Ada does not distinguish those
  declarations and references that involve shared
  data, the application system writer might not be
  aware that sharing is occurring. An entry call of
  another task is much more visible. (Although its
  syntax is that of a procedure call and indeed an
  entry can be renamed as a procedure, an entry call
  cannot be buried in an expression, unlike the use
  of a shared variable.)
- There is no explicit mutual-exclusion protocol to
  cope with conflicting individual accesses to the
  object. (Even a single Ada assignment will in
  general translate into several machine
  instructions in the case of record or array
  objects.)
- The memory containing the data objects might not
  be directly accessible to all the processors that
  execute the tasks that access the object.

- If processors of different types access the data there might be a problem with arranging a suitable representation of the data.
- The data might appear at different addresses for each processor.
- It could interact with task rendezvous. If all data is private to a task then it does not matter whether entry call parameters are copied at the time of the entry call or at the time of the corresponding accept , or if in or in out parameters are used by reference. Similarly consistent effects are achieved with parameters that are access objects. If however another task can change the data of the calling task while it is suspended on an entry call or during the rendezvous then the parameter-passing semantics are relevant.

The first, second and last problems also arise with non-distributed systems. Ideally shared data would not be used, since making the data private to a server task handling access to it is conceptually clearer and more secure. However for performance reasons, some applications will not be prepared to accept the overheads of this, and it is often necessary to minimise the periods of mutual exclusion, principally to allow concurrent read accesses. (For example, a process control system might have a 'plant database' recording its overall state, which needs to be examined frequently and efficiently by several tasks.) The application system writer must be aware of the first and last problems, although potentially an analyser tool could help by highlighting shared data and references to it.

The second problem is also the responsibility of the user, who must devise a specific protocol for access to each group of shared data objects. Obviously the construction system cannot detect errors in the use of such protocols. A user-written protocol will also achieve logical

sequences of accesses with the correct mutual-exclusion
during modification or prevention of modification during
examination.

It is not reasonable to expect the construction
system to handle the third problem (of data in a remote
memory). The reason is that shared data should normally
only be used where performance requirements dictate this.
This means that the memory holding the shared data must be
directly accessible. If this solution is not available for
an application, i.e. some of the accessing tasks must be
remote, then shared data is probably less efficient than
having a server task. The delay on a single access of a
shared variable is no worse than that which would occur with
the corresponding rendezvous but, in a logical operation
involving a series of accesses, the total delay could be
much worse since a transaction will occur for each access.
In contrast, if the operation is performed by an entry call,
the only transactions are those necessary to set up the
rendezvous and to transfer the parameters. So where there
are remote tasks a server task should be set up to handle
their requests, with the server task and local tasks using
shared data.

Therefore the construction system will probably
insist that shared data is in shared memory, i.e. directly
accessible to all processors that execute the tasks that
operate on it.

Sometimes the fourth problem, of arranging a
suitable common representation of the data to be used by all
processors, can be handled by the use of representation
clauses in the Ada source to prevent the application of the
default representation of the different compiler back-ends.
Each back-end must be clever enough to recognise where a
representation clause is the same as its default, to avoid
generating unnecessary conversion code. However this is not
in general sufficient: representation clauses do not give
total control over the representation.

The construction system must ensure that shared
data resides at the same addresses in the address space(s)

of each processor that addresses it. This is because the data might contain internal pointers (addresses).

It is impractical for the construction system to analyse the whole program on every compilation to determine which data is shared; hence the application system writer must deal specifically with shared data when allocating the software to the target configuration.

In summary most of the responsibility of dealing with the potential problems of shared data falls on the user rather than the construction system.

(ii) Shared code

This does not present the same problems as shared data since Ada code is inherently re-entrant with each thread of control having its own copy of local variables. (There will be only one copy of any data in the specification or outermost declarative part of the body of a library package; the user will be aware of this and presumably have his own protocols to avoid trouble.) There is still the possibility that the memory containing the code might not be addressable by the processor running a task. The simplest solution is to avoid this possibility in one of the following ways:

- The designer could arrange for shared memory to contain the shared code and allocate the code accordingly. Like shared data it must reside at the same addresses in the address space(s) of each processor that executes it, unless the compilers generate position-independent code.
- The designer could make the code into a separate task, where the callable procedures become entries of this task. The code could then be remote from some or all of the callers but the ability to have several concurrent executions is lost.
- The construction system could replicate the code locally to each calling task. This possibility is not available if there is data that is not local to the code since this will be shared data. As

discussed above, the construction system will
insist that this data is in directly-addressable
memory. This means that a replicated shared
library package must not have data in its
specification or in the outermost declarative part
of its body.

An alternative possibility is that the
construction system could arrange a remote-execution
mechanism. This is probably too complex but merits the brief
discussion that follows in the next few paragraphs.

Sharing the code by remote-execution is nontrivial since it is in principle executed by the calling
task and any local data ought to be allocated from the
resources of the calling task. Also several concurrent
executions of a given section of code might be in progress
at once.

One way to do remote-execution is for the
construction system to generate an implicit server task for
each possible remote caller. The application system writer
would have to specify the callers at build-time to avoid
extensive (or impossible) analysis because of the
possibility of run-time assignment to task access objects.
The server task would be executed on a processor that can
address the code. It would have its own stacks and heap.

If library packages do not contain data in their
specification (i.e. there is no shared data) they will
present a purely procedural interface. This is also the case
with library subprograms. Thus if one library package (or
subprogram) shared by remote-execution references another
there is no inherent problem. The builder must detect cases
where an implicit server task must be generated to deal with
calls by other implicit server tasks. This is easily
established from the with dependencies between library
units.

With this method, calls of procedures shared by
remote-execution become calls of entries of other tasks.
This avoids complicating the run-time system. Of course the

writer could arrange a similar task structure explicitly but
this would mean that the target configuration is reflected
in the Ada source, which is not desirable.

(iii) Shared task type code

Another form of sharing arises when several tasks
of a given Ada type are executing on the same processor. The
Ada source code for each task is the same, so one copy of
the corresponding object code would normally be shared by
the tasks. Some tasks which are instances of a task type
might only rendezvous with "close" neighbours, others might
rendezvous with "distant" tasks. If these tasks share the
code associated with the task type, the code compiled for a
rendezvous must be the same regardless of the underlying
implementation of the rendezvous (via shared memory, a
communications line, etc.).

A similar form of sharing could arise if the task
code is in a shared memory addressable by more than one
processor executing tasks of the type.

5.5 DISCUSSION OF THE POSSIBLE APPROACHES

Having examined the problems of option A, we can
now return to discussing the possible approaches introduced
in section 5.3.

From the discussion of the problems of sharing, it
emerges that this approach, "full Ada, one program", could
only be undertaken with horrendous implications for the
target system performance, and for the Apse support tools.

Approach B, "full Ada, multiple programs", is
certainly feasible; indeed in the absence of support from
the Apse and in target run-time systems, this is the only
approach that can be pursued.

The distributed software system would be defined
as a set of different programs, each intended for a
particular processor of the target system; in particular,
interprocessor communication channels would be handled at
the user program level like normal I/O devices.

Although early distributed systems will no doubt
be programmed using this approach, we advise strongly that
this is not a reasonable approach for the long term because:

1) the user must deal with low-level functions (like
   interprocessor channel handling) which depend on
   the target configuration only;
2) any change of the configuration of the target or
   of the software allocation may force the software
   design to be changed;
3) the language system cannot check fully the
   interfaces between programs, notably parameter
   types, in the same way as it checks the interfaces
   between tasks.

To allow a single (application-dependent only) Ada
program to be supported by a distributed system, it is
necessary to avoid sharing of data and code among physical
nodes of the target. Our possible approaches C and D
correspond to the two ways of achieving this restriction:

C) A restricted subset of Ada is forced both on
   tightly and loosely connected processors.
   (Communication between tasks is always restricted
   to entry calls without allowing sharing of data).
D) Full Ada is allowed only for tightly coupled
   processors. For loosely connected processors,
   communication is restricted to entry calls.

Approach C requires that the compiler (or a
preprocessor) checks for constructs outside the defined
subset; any program can be allocated in any way on the
distributed target. However, the approach introduces quite
severe limitations on the software even within a physical
node. Approach D is less restrictive.

We thus favour approach D. It can be supported in
two different ways:

D1) allocation directives are checked by the system
after compilation to prevent illegal communication
between tasks allocated to loosely connected
processors (in this way a program previously
validated by the compiler can become illegal at
allocation-time);

D2) a new concept (to be called from now on <u>virtual
node</u>) is introduced on top of Ada programs. A
virtual node is a set of one or more tasks and/or
packages, defined in full Ada, making only entries
visible to the outside world and being able to
call entries made visible by other virtual nodes.
A virtual node can be considered also as the
software allocation unit, allocated to physical
nodes.

The main difference between these two is that, in
the second case, the user is <u>aware</u> of designing a
distributed program; when the overall structure of the
program is defined, restrictions associated with
distribution are confined to the interactions between
virtual nodes.

In case D1, on the other hand, the programmer
works under the ideal assumption that the target is a single
memory computer, only to discover a little time later that
some perfectly valid constructions are rejected because of
allocation constraints.

In practice the programmer would learn how to
avoid such rejection, by anticipating possible distribution
at design time. So case D1 would degenerate into D2, but
without explicit system support for this way of designing.

Through the virtual node concept a programmer can
conceive a distributed program as a set of abstract nodes,
each of which performs a meaningful role for its
application. In other words, the virtual node concept can
be used also as a design tool; it is a modular unit which
provides controlled access to a set of resources. Many
virtual nodes may cooperate to provide a subsystem that

matches some specific functional requirements of the
application. On the other hand, approach Dl does not
provide any support for designing distributed programs; it
will not be investigated further.

5.6 VIRTUAL NODES

The virtual node concept is similar to language
constructs introduced in some recent proposals of concurrent
languages for distributed environments, like that of
"guardian" of extended CLU (Liskov 1982) and of ARGUS
(Liskov 1984), or that of "network-module" of *MOD (Bentley
1980), or others proposed by Downes & Goldsack (1980),
Andrews (1981), and Ghezzi (1982).

One way of thinking about a virtual node is as an
abstraction of a physical node: a virtual node supports one
or more tasks sharing memory and communicates with other
virtual nodes only by entry calls.

The ideal program development methodology
previously introduced may now be reconsidered with respect
to the virtual node concept (see also Figure 5.6A). It will
consist of the following actions:

1) decompose the application into a set of virtual
   nodes;
2) correct the program both within each virtual node
   and between them;
3) describe physical nodes and their interconnection
   links;
4) allocate virtual nodes to physical nodes.

Note that more than one virtual node can be
allocated to the same physical node. In such a case, for
efficiency reasons, communications among these nodes can be
implemented in the same way as the communication between
tasks within a single virtual node.

Note moreover that the virtual node concept would
not be embedded in the language itself, because this would
contravene the Ada standard; this means that the user cannot
be forced to follow this ideal methodology. In principle, it

is possible to follow another program development process, as depicted in Figure 5.6B.

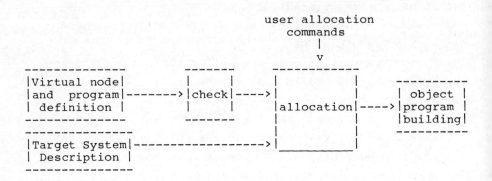

Figure 5.6A

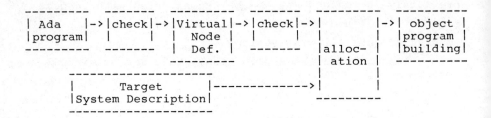

Figure 5.6B

This second process may be useful when an Ada program, that was written without knowledge of the distributed nature of the target, must be supported by a distributed system. In such a case, the virtual node construct allows the a posteriori functional decomposition of the program and allows checking of the correctness of inter-node communications without having to rewrite the unchanged parts of the program.

A virtual node could be defined in two different ways:

1) introducing a special declaration in the source
   text of the program to be recognised by the
   compiler or a preprocessor;
2) introducing a special declaration in a separate
   document to be processed by a special tool.

The second way is preferable because it allows
both the program development methodologies of Figures 5.6A
and 5.6B, avoiding any temporal dependency between Ada
program construction, virtual node description and checking.
We will subsequently assume this way of defining virtual
nodes; it is depicted in Figure 5.6C.

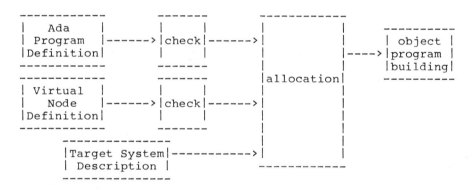

Figure 5.6C

Before ending this general discussion on the
virtual node concept (which will be expanded into a proposal
in the next chapters), we must deal with one more topic
related to implementation issues. At this point of
discussion it is not clear if the virtual node concept can
be automatically handled by the system or if other forms of
user activity are needed to create the distributed image of
the object program. This problem will be addressed later
with particular regard to the goal of limiting changes to
existing Apses.

What we would like to note here is that, even if
no automatic implementation is possible, the virtual node
approach allows us to keep the application software design
and development completely separate from any activity

related to the operation needed to have the program
supported by the distributed target.

For the sake of completeness, we note that the
virtual node is a concept superimposed on Ada programs.
Until now, the virtual node has been viewed largely as a
constraint. However, one could provide different semantics
for inter-node communication. For example, two virtual nodes
could interact through message-passing primitives rather
than by rendezvous. The model of communication between
virtual nodes could in principle be selected in such a way
that internode communication can be completely implemented
in Ada. Such an approach guarantees automatic
implementation of virtual nodes. On the other hand, it
implies the use of two different communication semantics:
one for communication within a node and one for
communication among nodes. The introduction of a specific
communication semantic for inter-node communication is
proposed by several authors who consider the rendezvous
mechanism not suited to distributed systems, see Ghezzi
(1982) and Rossi & Zicari (1982). Such an extension however
limits the portability of the program to different targets
(non distributed) and increases virtual node redefinition
effort.

5.7 AN EXAMPLE APPLICATION OF VIRTUAL NODES

To illustrate the virtual node approach, let us
consider again the example system for dish washer production
lines (example 5 of Chapter 2).

Recall the functions of the system. Each
manufactured appliance travels on an assembly line while
measurements are executed on its functioning. At the end of
each line, measurements from single machines are collected
and analyzed, and the attendants are warned. Data from
several such lines are sent to a central location where
statistics and reports are prepared if necessary.

The functions can be referred to as follows:

a. measurement and control of moving products;

b. analysis of collected measurements for a single product:

c. warning attendants;

d. analysis of information for a single line;

e. collection and analysis of data from the whole plant.

A reasonable grouping of the functions into virtual nodes is the following:

$$
\begin{array}{lll}
& a + b + c: & \text{machine supervisor} \\
(1) & d & : \quad \text{line supervisor} \\
& e & : \quad \text{central monitor}
\end{array}
$$

This organisation is a neat partition of the tasks so that data flow between partitions (i.e. virtual nodes) is minimal, and can be conveniently achieved by entry calls. However, physical constraints have to be considered too, which dictate that the microprocessors accompanying the products be the simplest possible, and that communication with attendants be conveyed to a central giant display. Accordingly, tasks b. and c. are withdrawn from the first node and added to the line supervisor, resulting in the following partition:

$$
\begin{array}{lll}
& a & : \quad \text{machine supervisor;} \\
(2) & b + c + d: & \text{line supervisor;} \\
& e & : \quad \text{central monitor.}
\end{array}
$$

This partition defines a central monitor and two families of identical virtual nodes: one family consists of as many machine supervisors as there are products; the other family consists of as many line supervisors are there are lines in the plant. Apart from their identification, members of a family are essentially identical programs. (This shows the importance of having in the language some means to instantiate several instances of the same source code.)

A straightforward hardware implementation would use separate computers for each virtual node; communication between travelling computers and their line supervisor is by infra-red links.

To use this example to illustrate the flexibility of the virtual node approach, now assume that the same computer is assigned two or more lines to supervise. Then the corresponding virtual nodes of family "line supervisor" would be allocated to the same computer. Since these nodes have much common source code, the construction system should arrange for code sharing. Notice that the change of virtual node allocation does not require any changes to the source program.

Finally the computer hardware on the dish washer could become multiprocessor for enhanced computing power, if more tests had to be performed on the product. Such a change of target configuration would not affect the source program (apart of course from the newly implemented tests); the construction system should automatically reconfigure the object code for the new configuration.

5.8 SUMMARY

We have described why we favour the "virtual node" approach to designing distributed systems written in Ada.

In this approach, the system is written as a single Ada program. The program is partitioned by the user into virtual nodes, which are groups of tasks communicating only by rendezvous. Within the virtual node, there are no restrictions on the use of Ada.

We separate the stages of software system design (including virtual node definition) and of software allocation to the physical target (including mapping of virtual nodes onto physical nodes); this allows reallocation when the target configuration alters, without software redesign.

The approach involves no change to the Ada language. Restrictions on the ways Ada is used, and software allocation, are accomplished in the Apse.

6

Detailed consideration of the construction system

6.1 INTRODUCTION

This chapter considers the detailed problems that must be addressed by a construction system for building application systems written in Ada for distributed targets. Chapter 7 considers the implementation of this within the Apse.

Processors are regarded as having a virtual to physical address mapping scheme, via an associated memory-mapping unit (MMU). Processors without address translation are special cases where there is only one possible mapping. The construction system discussed here does not require processors to have address translation, but it allows some of the target's processors to have such mapping.

The term "compilation domain" or "domain" is used instead of the Ada reference manual term "library file".

6.2 OBJECTIVES FOR THE CONSTRUCTION SYSTEM

The first step in producing a construction system for distributed targets is to determine the additional major objectives for the construction system arising out of the nature of the targets. There are three objectives:

(i) Coping with the distribution.

The potential distribution of the target includes not only the immediately apparent physical distribution, with processors connected via data-transmission links, but also configurations where, for example, the bottleneck of multi-processor traffic on a single bus is avoided by tightly coupling several buses via memories accessible from more than one bus. Thus a system could have many processors

and many memories and usually most (if not all) processors
will not be able to access all the memories.

Figures 6.1 to 6.4 illustrate the variety of
configurations that might occur in practice. In these
examples, "P" represents a processor, and "M" a memory.

Figure 6.1
A centralised multi-
processor system

Figure 6.2
Two groups of hardware
with a communications link

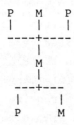

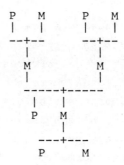

Figure 6.3
Fast communication
between buses via a
dual-ported memory

Figure 6.4
A tightly-coupled system with no
memory addressable by all processors

This chapter therefore deals with a generalised
hardware configuration, encompassing all the specific
architectures described in Chapter 2.

A second objective is to recognise the flexibility
in the choice of the target hardware configuration and in
the allocation of the software to it and therefore:

(ii) Supporting reconfiguration or re-allocation
without requiring the user or system to change the
Ada source of the application system or to perform
a lengthy regeneration of the run-time system.

This objective means that, where possible, the Ada source should not refer to the target hardware, or make assumptions about it. In particular, the construction system should not require configuration or allocation information to be specified in the Ada source (e.g. via pragmas).

A minor objective is:

(iii) Not to require all processing of Ada source to be repeated on re-configuration or re-allocation.

This is minor because it merely saves machine resources in a relatively infrequent operation.

6.3 BASIC ASSUMPTIONS

The design of any construction system will require choices to be made about how to handle certain problems and choices of restrictions to be imposed to eliminate problems or undesirable interaction between solutions to problems. It is impossible to discuss the construction system without effectively making some of these decisions.

Three basic assumptions are made in this chapter:

(i) Construction is entirely an offline process; i.e. there is no run-time re-configuration or re-allocation.

This is assumed in the design of Ada, which expects extensive compile-time checking whose time and space overhead could not be afforded at run-time.

Systems with dynamic re-configuration or re-allocation can be written in Ada, but they will require greater target resources to allow the run-time system to perform (or complete) jobs, including Ada checking, that are usually done offline.

This decision does not rule out a simple type of fault-tolerant system in which the software can detect failure of a hardware component and cease using it until it is replaced by identical hardware. Another possibility is the provision of standby components used after a fault.

Allocation will be entirely offline except for that of nested tasks to processors. Even here, the

construction system will determine the set of eligible
processors.

Chapter 8 does consider systems with more dynamic
reconfiguration.

(ii) The construction system considered here will
address the problems of generating code that can
be directly executed by the target processors.

Early construction systems might well generate
pseudo-code for a standard conceptual target, with this code
being interpreted at run-time. (Indeed this approach is
probably the only viable solution for 8-bit processors.)
This pseudo-code approach avoids several of the problems
that this study addresses, at the cost of run-time speed.

(iii) The use of the virtual node (VN) approach to
achieve the objectives of 6.1.

The VN concept has already been introduced. The
next section describes in detail what constitutes a VN, the
software restrictions, and the hardware support needed.

6.4 VIRTUAL NODES AND RELATED PROBLEMS

A virtual node (VN) has been defined in Chapter 5
as a group of one or more Ada tasks that are logically
related. The assignment to groups should be determined by
the user on the basis of the functions the application
system is to perform, not by the hardware.

The tasks that are grouped by the user to form a
VN are selected from the set of 'outermost-level' tasks of
the program; i.e. the 'task' that executes the main
subprogram and the tasks that are activated during initial
elaboration of the program (those in the specification of a
library package or in the outermost declarative part of the
body of a library package). Nested tasks can be considered
as part of the VN of the ancestor 'outermost task'.

The code of a task comprises all the code that the
task could directly execute. It thus includes any
referenced library package or subprogram code as well as
that of the task body. Similarly the data of a task is all
the data that the task could directly access, including data

in the library packages referenced by the task.

The principal restriction imposed by the virtual
node approach is that the application system will be
partitioned into groups of tasks. The construction system
will not support the use of data (static, stack-based or
heap-based) or code shared between VNs. (The restriction on
shared code means that one copy of the code cannot be shared
between VNs. Of course each VN can have its own copy of the
code provided this does not violate the data-sharing
restriction. This will arise frequently because of the use
of Ada library packages.)

Within a VN the construction system will insist on
shared memory to hold code or data shared between tasks of
the VN. This restriction avoids the complexities involved
in providing mechanisms, such as automatically-generated
server tasks, for remote shared data and remote shared code.
('Remote' means that the processor executing the task
accessing the data or executing the code cannot address the
memory containing it.)

In the case of shared data there can only be one
copy but shared code can be replicated to conform to the
restriction on sharing one copy (and to reduce requirements
for shared memory).

In fact the restriction that data shared between
tasks must be directly addressable by the processors
executing the tasks is not onerous. A mechanism for remote
shared data might well be less efficient than a rendezvous
interface to a server task for the data. This is because
each access to remote shared data would involve delay,
whereas a single rendezvous may perform a number of
logically related operations on a collection of data.

This implementation of the virtual node approach
only requires a communication path between two processors
executing tasks that need to rendezvous. This could be via
shared memory or via a communications line between buses.
Whether this path must be direct or indirect (via other
processors) is considered later.

Subsequent discussion will show that the cases of rendezvous within a VN and rendezvous between two VNs are very similar.

Hardware Nodes

It is useful to introduce the concept of a hardware node. This is a named subset of the target configuration. Its primary purpose is to be a more convenient way of referring to a particular part of the target, than individual processors, memories and so on.

VNs are mapped onto hardware nodes, allowing the construction system to perform default allocation of tasks to processors and code and data to memories. The concept of a hardware node is most useful if some restriction is made on its hardware content, to provide the minimum requirements of a VN.

The intuitive idea of a hardware node is that its component processors and memories are tightly-coupled. However, if the run-time system provides a general inter-processor routing service it is not necessary that nodes have to be composed of contiguous components. For example two processors in a node might have to communicate via other processors not in the node. However each memory must be addressable by at least one processor in the node.

It is not necessary that nodes be disjoint; memories and processors can be in more than one node. This allows code-sharing between VNs and the mapping of tasks from different VNs onto the same processor.

This would have the major benefit that the sharing of one copy of some code by more than one VN could be attained if the particular configuration allowed this optimisation. This would mean that the VN structure of an application system would not need to be re-defined to achieve this sharing. (Note that this does not conflict with the VN restrictions, because the construction system is not required to support such sharing but merely to do it if possible.)

The problem of heap partitions

A design choice is whether to insist that all
tasks of a VN use the same heap partition or to allow
several partitions in a VN.

The single heap partition restriction simplifies
the run-time system but has these disadvantages:

- There must be a memory to hold the heap partition
  that can be addressed by all the processors used
  by a VN; this is a major constraint on the
  hardware configuration.
- The representation of objects in the heap must be
  suitable for all types of processor accessing it.
- In particular, unless all processors of the VN
  have the same addressing style, the contents of
  access objects cannot be simple virtual addresses.

So we recommend that the construction system allow
several heap partitions within a VN. The construction
system can then make the reasonable restriction that all
processors that use a given heap partition must be of the
same type and must use the same part of their address space
to map it.

A number of points are introduced by allowing
several heap partitions for a VN:

- How the user should declare and use heap
  partitions.
- The possibility of references between heap
  partitions.
- Static (library package) data structures can
  reference heap objects. Any processor that must
  be able to address a given static data structure
  must also be able to address any heap partitions
  that it references. If heap references are
  involved, the processors that access the static
  data structure must be of the same type, because
  of the restriction above.

-   It cannot be simply assumed that access objects
    can be parameters (directly or indirectly) of
    rendezvous between tasks of a VN.

Considering the first point, the probable method
would be for the user to declare which heap partition is to
be used for objects of each access type. This would be done
via a pragma in the same declarative part, which associates
the type name with a logical partition name. (There would
be a default name for type declarations without pragmas.) At
allocation-time each logical partition will be mapped onto a
memory. The construction system will allow more than one
logical partition to be mapped onto the same physical heap
partition.

The code generated from declarations of access
objects must identify the logical heap partition, to inform
the run-time system.

If an access type is used in more than one VN
(perhaps by being declared in a library package) then one
logical partition name will be mapped into one physical
partition for each VN. (The construction system will not
support data structures shared between VNs.)

Considering the second point, the construction
system can determine from the type declarations which types
will cause references between logical heap partitions, (e.g.
when an access type references another access type.) These
logical partitions might not be mapped onto the same
physical heap partition. If so, a processor that deals with
objects of the type would have to be able to address more
than one heap partition. This partially re-introduces a
hardware constraint removed by provision of several heap
partitions for a VN.

Where an access type involves discriminated record
types the construction system will have to consider all the
access types mentioned in the variant parts.

A feasible approach would be to allow references
between physical heap partitions but to insist that where
this occurs any processor that can address one of the
partitions must also be able to address the other. This

would allow situations like:

```
    ----------              ----------              ----------
    I        I              I        I              I        I
    I   A    I---------->I  B     I              I   C    I
    I        I              I        I              I        I
    ----------              ----------              ----------
    I                          I    I                       I
    I                          I    I                       I
    I                          I    I                       I
    I        --------          I    I          -------       I
    I        I      I          I    I          I     I       I
    ------I  P1  I------      -------I  P2  I------
             I      I                      I     I
             --------                      -------
```

Heap partition B would hold access objects of
types useful to processors P1 and P2, whereas partitions A
and C would contain objects of a type local to the tasks
executing on processor P1 or P2 respectively.

The third point (of static data referencing heap
objects) is a restriction that must be observed by the user.
Obviously there is scope for declaring a heap partition
purely to hold access objects associated with a given static
data structure. This partition can then be allocated to the
same memory as the static part of the structure. This would
often require access types to be derived (in the Ada sense)
so they can be allocated to such a partition. The
construction system must check the addressability constraint
is satisfied by all processors that operate on the data
structure. It will use the relevant object type
declarations to do this.

Considering the fourth point, if two processors
can address the memory containing the relevant heap
partition there is no problem with access objects, either
directly as rendezvous parameters or contained in composite
objects that are rendezvous parameters. If the construction
system will arrange that a heap partition occupies the same
addresses for all processors that use it, then the contents
of access objects can be passed as virtual addresses. (Note
that heap objects can only refer to other heap objects, and
not to static data structures so there will be no references

outside the heap address space.)

The single exception to the above will be to allow
task access objects to be passed in any rendezvous. This is
necessary to allow the pattern of task communication to be
changed at run-time, and to overcome the asymmetry of the
rendezvous mechanism where the called task does not
automatically know the identity of the caller. Task access
objects are special in that they are not actually pointers
to other user-defined objects. They only appear to be like
other access objects because of the Ada design decision to
make tasks look like data objects.

6.5 TASK ALLOCATION
a) Constraints on allocation of tasks to processors

'Outermost-level' tasks will be allocated to
processors by the construction system. One such task is the
'task' that executes the main subprogram, and other tasks
may be created during initial elaboration of library
packages before entry into the main subprogram.

One reason for this decision is that the
allocation of tasks to processors is the major factor that
determines the allocation of code and data to memories and
also vice versa. There is thus a circularity. This is not
a problem for a system with run-time allocation of both
tasks and code and data. However it is a basic assumption
that code and data is allocated offline. It is difficult
for the construction system to decide where to put code and
data without any idea of where tasks will run, i.e. without
an explicit description by the user of the distributed
target topology and organisation. (The user could decide
this, but would lose the possibility of automated allocation
by the construction system.)

Secondly, if little or nothing is known about
where tasks will run it is impossible for the construction
system to perform the necessary extensive checking of
adherence to allocation constraints. This includes checking
that tasks that are allocated a logical channel are
allocated to either end of it, that a task that handles an

interrupt is allocated to the processor that generates the
interrupt, and that there will be a processor of the right
type that can address the code and data of a task.   To
perform such checks dynamically would be a major burden for
the run-time system; as well as the size implications, there
are problems of access to the relevant information in the
compilation domain, such as symbol tables and a convenient
representation of the program.

In summary, offline allocation of outermost-level
tasks to processors is needed to allow the construction
system to allocate code and data, rather than requiring
detailed instructions from the user, and to allow the
construction system to perform allocation constraint
checking, rather than requiring the run-time system to do
it.

Outermost-level tasks, although created
dynamically, will not normally terminate in control
applications.   They will be used for the major functions of
the application system and hence must be carefully
allocated.   The construction system must therefore allow the
user to specify constraints on their allocation, to the
point of specifying the exact processor if need be.

However it is not necessary to insist that nested
tasks are allocated offline.   (These nested tasks are
created and terminated during execution of the application
system.) This section considers the constraints on the
dynamic allocation of nested tasks imposed by the Ada
definition.   (There are other constraints arising from the
possible use of different types of hardware.)

Tasks can be dynamically created by a parent task
either by elaboration of a nested task object declaration or
by use of an allocator to assign to a task access object.
The primary constraint on allocation is not determined by
the method of creation of a task but rather by whether the
task type declaration is nested or not.

Tasks created from nested task type declarations

Ada allows task type declarations to be nested within other code i.e. effectively within the code of another task type. This means that any task of the nested type can execute code that is visible in the context of the nested task type declaration, and can access the data of other tasks that is similarly visible. Some of this data could be dynamic; i.e. stack-based or heap-based. This causes an intimate binding between a parent task and its offspring tasks. (A strict hierarchy is enforced, however, because the type declaration is not visible outside the code of the parent and hence only the parent can create tasks of the type.)

A principal benefit of tasks created from nested task type declarations is to arrange the inheritance of the context of the parent at little run-time cost. Therefore it is reasonable to conclude that a nested task has to run on the same type of processor as the parent. This avoids the principal problem of arranging a suitable representation of data of ancestor tasks that is referenced by the nested task and the lesser problem of arranging versions in different instruction sets of shared code.

The construction system can determine at allocation-time the set of processors eligible to run the tasks of a given nested task type dynamically created by a given outermost-level task. Each of these processors must be able to address:
- the code and data of the nested task,
- the stacks, heap and data structures of the ancestor tasks that are referenced by the nested task type declaration,
- similarly for the visible code of ancestor tasks that is referenced by the nested task type declaration.

This requires task type information to be available at run-time in calls to the run-time system to create a task. Also for each task type the set of eligible processors must be part of the run-time system data.

Tasks created from non nested task type declarations

When the task type declaration is not nested in
the code of the parent task (i.e. it is made visible by the
library package mechanism) a nested task has a limited
connection with the parent: the parent has no control over
the task except to abort it (or request a rendezvous). It
can however request information about it:
- whether it is callable (attribute CALLABLE)
- whether it is terminated (attribute TERMINATED)
- the number of calls queued on a given entry
  (attribute COUNT)
- the parent is delayed on exit from the scope in
  which the nested task was declared (or the access
  type was declared, in the case of a task access
  object) until the task exits.

These attributes have fairly precise semantics in
a shared environment; their meaning is not so clear in a
distributed one, where the time to obtain the information
may be significant, and the state of the task may change
during that time.

There is no inherent constraint on the set of
processors that can run a task created from an un-nested
task type declaration apart from the obvious ones (see
below). Task type information must be available at run-time,
as with tasks from nested type declarations. The run-time
system must support communication between the processors of
the task and those of its parent task and other calling
tasks. This will be a constraint if the run-time system
does not provide general inter-processor routing.

Of course, the eligible processors are determined
by which versions of the task in different instruction sets
there are (determined by the user) and the addressability by
a processor of the version of the task's code relevant to
it. There might be more than one copy of some or all of the
code of a task type.

User-determined allocation constraints

The user might wish to impose constraints on allocation of tasks, whether or not their task type declaration is nested and whether or not tasks are nested or outermost-level. This could be:

- a restriction on all tasks of a given task type;
- the same for all tasks of the type created within a given outermost-level task;
- a restriction on all tasks created from a given task object or task access object declaration.

The use of such constraints would be to confine the load of a given system function to one part of the target, or to ensure that an adequate (e.g. 16-bit or more) processor was used to give suitable performance.

The user can easily name task type, task object or task access object declarations, because these appear at definable places in the Ada source. Some tasks can be anonymous, for example with creation via an allocator of one or more tasks in an executable statement, but the user can obviously avoid this if a name is needed.

b) Allocation of nested tasks

When the part of the run-time system responsible for a processor must create a nested task it will be aware of the set of processors, including its own, that are eligible to run the task. (This will be determined before run-time, as above.) However it will not be aware of the current loading of these processors since they will in general be running nested tasks allocated from elsewhere in the target. (In a decentralised run-time system no one part has an overview of what is happening elsewhere.) Therefore if the run-time system for the processor of the parent task wishes to allocate a new task to another processor it must request the run-time system of that processor to accept it. The requested processor run-time system will decide whether it can take the new task in addition to its current load. It will probably only consider the number of tasks it has, rather than the number that are currently active. If any more subtle algorithm is needed, during construction the

user will have to specify some quantification of the
resource requirements of tasks of a given type (CPU usage,
memory needed, and so on).

So the process of allocation will be one where the
run-time system responsible for the parent task will request
other processor run-time systems in turn to accept the new
task, until a request is successful. If the run-time
systems for all the eligible processors have rejected the
request, the new task would have to be run on the same
processor as its parent or the run-time system could try
again later, delaying the parent task.

If a processor run-time system accepts a request
it will consider the new task as part of its load, even
though it will need follow-up information from the
requesting run-time system to set up the task control block
and so on. This avoids any problems caused by new requests
arriving before creation of the new task is complete.

The requesting run-time system will create the
task object (or task access object) in the parent to contain
the identity of the processor whose run-time system accepted
it. (This object is the user-defined data object referring
to the task and is not part of the run-time system data
structure for a task.)

Once a task has been accepted it cannot be re-
allocated to another processor part-way through its
execution. If this were allowed there would be problems
caused by tasks operating with the old task object (or task
access object) contents after the task had been re-allocated
but before the object had been updated (or vice versa).
Since it is desirable to allow the contents of such objects
to be passed around the system freely, via rendezvous or
shared data, there could be multiple copies in distinct
memories with no processor able to address all copies.

However there is at least one special case. If
there are several identical processors on one bus the run-
time system might have a single part to deal with the set as
a whole, rather than one part for each processor. In this
case the run-time system could re-allocate between its

processors without affecting its interface to the rest of
the run-time system.

6.6 PACKAGES STANDARD AND SYSTEM

The construction system for a distributed target
must take one of two basic approaches to these packages:
(i) adhere to a single definition of each package, or
(ii) allow multiple definitions.

In either case it is clear that MEMORY_SIZE in
package SYSTEM (giving the total memory size) is not useful
for a distributed target. The construction system will be
informed of memory sizes during the specification of the
target configuration, but it will not support use of these
sizes by application system code; e.g. there will be no
special mechanism to detect references to MEMORY_SIZE in the
Ada source.

If approach (i) is used the user would have to
accept that the use of different types of processor will
involve conversion time and space overheads for processors
that cannot operate on values with the predefined length.
(There are other problems, discussed later.) This
inefficiency could be overcome by the definition of derived
types and the use of representation clauses on them to give
values of an appropriate representation. However this would
embed knowledge of the target hardware into the Ada source.

Approach (i) would also imply that only one type
of predefined hardware address is available. Again derived
types with representation clauses would allow addresses of
different formats for different processor-MMU combinations
but would embed target knowledge in the Ada source.

Thus approach (i) is only acceptable for
application systems with homogeneous target hardware.

Approach (ii) would allow the definition of
several versions of the specification of packages STANDARD
and SYSTEM, each with an appropriate body. All the
compilation units that contribute towards the code of a task
would need to use the same version of each package.

Data interfaces between different definitions of
STANDARD and SYSTEM will occur at:
- shared data structures,
- rendezvous parameters passed by copy.

Both cases therefore need control of the internal
representation. This will be the case, as discussed later
in 6.7.3.

6.7 MAJOR DESIGN ISSUES FOR THE CONSTRUCTION SYSTEM

Now we have examined the main problem areas, we
can consider various important issues for the construction
system itself. These are:
- the stages of construction,
- implementation of task rendezvous,
- homogeneity of the hardware in a node,
- whether to offer a rendezvous routing service,
- generation of the run-time system,
- initial elaboration of the program,
- partial linking,
- code replication,
- symbolic debugging,
- the degree of automation.

These points are discussed in sections 6.7.1 to
6.7.1Ø respectively.

6.7.1 Stages of construction

The stages of construction will be:
- specifying the composition of VNs;
- processing each compilation unit with one or more
  compilers (depending on what different types of
  processor will execute code generated from the Ada
  source);
- specifying the target configuration;
- specifying the composition of nodes;
- specifying the allocation of VNs to nodes (or more
  detailed specification, depending on the degree of
  automation of the construction system);

- linking;
- configuring the run-time system and linking the run-time system to the user-written code if necessary;
- building an image file for each memory. Each file could include user-defined code and data, heap partitions, space for task stacks, a part of the run-time system code and data structures.

The degree of automation of the construction system will constrain the freedom to choose the order of these steps. (The more automated, the earlier configuration and allocation information is needed.)

6.7.2 Task rendezvous

The points to be discussed here are the method of passing parameters, the rendezvous mechanism, and the representation of parameter values.

a) Parameter-passing method

Parameters can be passed:

- by reference, i.e. merely passing the address of the data descriptor of each parameter object, or
- by copy, i.e. the value of each parameter object is passed.

The first method is usually more efficient, since composite objects can be large. However it relies on the ability of the processor that executes the called task to address the memories containing the objects referred to by the parameters.

It is important that rendezvous be as efficient as possible, whether between VNs or within a VN, and hence the aim should be to use reference semantics where possible. (Of course, for scalar objects, where a small amount of transmitted information is involved, copy semantics are mandatory.)

Individually, passing by copy and passing by reference are, in principle at least, straightforward. A design decision is involved, however, because there are situations where an entry call in the code could potentially

result in different parameter-passing methods on different
executions of the call. This arises with several tasks
sharing one copy of the code of a task type or an entry call
via a task access object, which can be re-assigned to refer
to another task between entry calls.

If the construction system can determine (after
allocation) that all executions can use call by reference
then it should do so and avoid the overhead of a run-time
decision. In practice this can only be done for entry calls
made on a named task (i.e. not via a task access object).

Further, the construction system can note
rendezvous where the parameters (directly or indirectly)
include access objects. For such rendezvous, reference
semantics should be used. Where the tasks involved in the
rendezvous are known at allocation-time the construction
system can report rendezvous that cannot be implemented by
reference. However, where task access objects are used any
error must be detected at run-time by the run-time system.

Another point is that reference semantics are only
possible where both processors are of the same type. (The
use, with different hardware types, of representation
clauses for all types of object in the rendezvous is not in
general sufficient, for reasons discussed below in the
section on the representation of rendezvous parameter
values.) Again, the construction system can perform this
analysis after allocation to determine when copy semantics
must be used for a given called task (but not necessarily
for all tasks that can be called via the entry call).

Similarly if access objects are involved the two
processors must be of the same type (or rather, addressing
format) because the contents of such objects will be virtual
addresses.

The problem remains of both copy and reference
semantics being needed on different executions of a given
entry call. The most promising approach is to arrange that
the run-time system makes the decision so that reference
semantics are used where possible.

This means that the Ada run-time system must have
knowledge of the general representation of data objects; i.e
it must understand data descriptors. The run-time system
must present a high-level rendezvous interface to the code
generated by the compiler, in which parameters are always
passed as references to data descriptors. The compiler will
therefore make no decision about the parameter-passing
semantics. It will generate code with reference semantics
for every entry call and every accept statement.

The run-time system will decide on each rendezvous
whether it is necessary to create local copies of the data
objects referenced by the parameters (unless the offline
analysis by the construction system has determined that
reference semantics can always be used for this entry call,
or that reference semantics must be used because access
objects are involved or that copy semantics must be used
because the processors are of different types).

To make the decision the run-time system for the
calling task will transmit a list of the memories referenced
by the parameters. This can be determined easily by the
run-time system from the addresses of the parameter objects,
and access type information recorded by the construction
system. For each parameter the construction system can
determine from its type which physical heap partition (if
any) is involved, or might be involved for discriminated
records. The construction system can then add to the
information associated with the entry call a list of heap
partitions that are (or might be) involved.

The run-time system for the called task can then
determine whether the processor of the called task can
address all these memories (using a list of addressable
memories determined by the construction system at
allocation-time). If not, copy semantics must be used. The
run-time system for the called task will thus select the
semantics. The rendezvous parameter area in the called task
will be set up to reference the original objects (for
reference) or local copies (for copy).

Since only copying is involved there is no need
for type information to be available at run-time for this
purpose.

References must be physical addresses (e.g. memory
number and offset within memory) rather than virtual ones,
since a mapping scheme is in general local to a processor.
The run-time system thus has the problem of arranging the
mapping for the called task to refer to the copied or
referenced parameter objects. (Access objects are not a
problem since if they are allowed in a rendezvous the two
processors must use the same part of their address space for
the same heap partition.)

The simplest solution where processors have
sufficient addressing capability is to allocate unique
addresses within each memory 'association'. (The set of
non-private memories that can be addressed by a given
processor is in the same 'association' as another set if the
two sets have at least one memory in common.)

If this is not possible then reference semantics
can only be used if the processor for the called task has a
suitable part of its address space unused at the time of the
call (and throughout execution of the accept statement). In
practice this requires some part of the address space to be
permanently reserved. Nested accept statements could lead
to exhaustion of such reserved address space, requiring copy
semantics for the more deeply nested rendezvous.

Call by reference does not introduce any extra
difficulties with sharing of data between processors.
Either a data object is private to the calling task, which
is suspended during the rendezvous, or it is shared with
other tasks, in which case the user should have devised a
protocol to arbitrate simultaneous access.

The run-time query to decide copy or reference
semantics does not involve extra communication, merely some
extra information, since a rendezvous between tasks
executing on different processors will require an opening
rendezvous request, with a response from the run-time system
for the called task.

Of course, the possibility of an exception in the called task during the rendezvous means that the use of reference semantics could leave the objects referenced by the rendezvous parameters in an uncertain state. The exception handler in the calling task must cope with this (if necessary) unless it is certain that copy semantics will always be used, regardless of the allocation.

b) Rendezvous mechanism

There do not appear to be any basic design decisions involved in this, except that a standard rendezvous protocol must be designed which is then mapped onto the particular communications protocol for the particular type of connection between the tasks. The communications software will present a standard interface to the rest of the run-time system to allow a clean separation between the rendezvous protocol and the mechanism of data transmission. (This might be via a communications line, a small shared memory for parameter-passing that can be addressed by both processors, etc.)

Implementation of the rendezvous requires a simple handshaking protocol between the two parts of the run-time system. In outline, the run-time system for the calling task will request a rendezvous. This request will contain a query whether copy or reference semantics should be used, or a statement that reference or copy semantics must be used. The receiving part of the run-time system will note the request and will respond when the corresponding accept is executed and this request is at the head of the queue. The calling part of the run-time system will then respond by transmitting parameter references or values or will respond with a timeout status to terminate the rendezvous attempt. Once the rendezvous has been set up in this way the rest is straightforward. At the end of the rendezvous the values of appropriate parameters or an exception number will be returned. Detection of errors in transmission and recovery from them is done by the lower-level communications protocol.

However this relatively simple arrangement will be complicated by:

- conditional entry calls, where the request will state that it is a conditional call and the run-time system for the called task will respond;
- nested _accept_ statements;
- communication failures that cannot be contained by the communications protocol;
- task abort during rendezvous;
- optimisations, e.g. reducing transmissions by passing parameter values or references in the initial rendezvous request, where the semantics have been decided offline by the construction system.

c) Representation of rendezvous parameter values

Where parameter values are passed between tasks that are executing on different types of processor, a problem of representation arises like that for shared data.

The simplest solution would be to require the user to give a representation clause for each type involved in such rendezvous. But since it is an objective to avoid reference to the target configuration in the Ada source this would require representation clauses for all types involved in any rendezvous. Another disadvantage is that this representation would apply to all objects of the types, resulting in inefficiency in all operations on such objects if the specified representation is not one of those supported by a particular processor's instruction set. A third problem is that representation clauses do not give total control over representation. For example the length in bits of integer values can be specified, but the ordering of bytes within the integer cannot, and this differs between types of processor.

A solution that involves passing details of representation in the transmitted values is impractical because of the inefficiency interpreting such details, compared to a call of a specific conversion routine.

Therefore the run-time system will need to convert values to either:

- the internal representation of the processor of the called task, or
- some standard form.

The latter involves two conversions (local_1-to-standard and standard-to-local_2). However it avoids the need for each processor run-time system to include multiple local-to-local conversion routines for all types of connected processor. It also provides a cleaner separation of processor run-time systems.

A conversion routine is needed for each type of object involved in rendezvous between different types of processor. The set of such object types can only be established after allocation. Where task access objects are involved the user will need to specify which rendezvous will not involve a different type of processor, otherwise the construction system must assume this.

A special tool, operating on the compiler output recorded in the domain, can establish the internal representation used (default or determined by a representation clause). The tool can therefore can generate the code of routines to convert values of each object type from the local internal representation to the standard form and vice versa. Alternatively it could decide no conversion was necessary.

The run-time system needs to be aware of the type of each object involved in such rendezvous, so that it knows which conversion routine to use. This information can be added by the tool to the code generated from entry calls and accept statements. Practical considerations of the difficulty in manipulating back-end output might require the compiler to generate type numbers, relocated by the linker, which are removed by the tool for rendezvous not between different processor types. Type declarations are static constructs and hence can be uniquely numbered offline.

The run-time system of the calling task will be aware of the type of processor executing the called task

because task objects and task access objects will contain
the processor number. Thus it can avoid conversion on
rendezvous where different types are not involved, even if
some executions of the rendezvous code are between different
processor types. (This relates to the problem of the code
of an entry call being shared by several tasks of a task
type or involving a task access object.)

Of course the standard form should be chosen to be
as compatible as possible with the default representations
for the different processor types. So the standard form
could be determined by the set of processor types in an
application system.

The conversion of values between different
representations might lead to slight loss of accuracy of
floating-point values.

6.7.3 Homogeneity of node hardware

A decision to be made by the construction system
designer is whether to cater for hardware of different types
in the same node. Reasons for allowing this include the
need for special processors and cost-effectiveness. The
problems introduced by heterogeneous hardware are:

(i) providing a suitable common representation of data
shared between tasks executing on different types
of processor in the same VN (and hence node).

(ii) a similar problem of potential conversion of the
representation of parameter values passed on
rendezvous between tasks in the same VN but
executing on different types of processor.

(iii) coping with the situation where some Ada source
could be shared by tasks except that they execute
on different types of processor

Problem (ii) arises anyway with rendezvous between
tasks in different nodes with different hardware. It should
be handled by the run-time system as described above.

The third problem is also not new since the same
situation could arise with homogeneous nodes but non-
homogeneous hardware overall. The Ada source must be

processed into code for more than one instruction set.

The Ada compilation domain must cope with several forms of compiler output for one compilation unit, dependent on different versions of packages STANDARD and SYSTEM. The processor type will be recorded as an attribute in the domain.

The construction system would need to check that all the compilation units linked for a given task had been compiled for the type of processor to which the task is allocated, and also that all the compilation units use the same versions of package STANDARD (and SYSTEM).

Thus only the sharing of data structures is a new problem introduced by heterogeneous hardware nodes. This situation is not really justifiable since shared data would normally be used as a high-performance interface between tasks, compared to a rendezvous interface. If conversion is involved in each access to the data the performance advantage is eroded; a rendezvous interface might be better.

If the problem is to be addressed, Ada representation clauses are not an entirely suitable solution, for the reasons given in 6.7.2 in considering the problem of rendezvous parameter value representation.

Thus a general solution would involve a form of 'representation clause' whereby the user specifies the set of types of processor that execute tasks that access a given shared data structure. Compilers would use a representation determined by this set. These representations would be determined by the compiler writers, as those of the pre-defined types, plus rules for the structure of composite objects (records or arrays) and for lengths of constrained types (where shorter representations could be used because of a limited range of values) and so on.

To be practical this might require constraints on which processor types could operate on the same data structure. This could for example limit the set to those from a family of processors from one manufacturer.

User specification of the types of processor operating on shared data is probably necessary because it

would be inconvenient for the construction system to
determine the static data structures that are shared between
tasks executing on different types of processor.

Firstly, the allocation would have to be specified
before compilation (before use of back-ends certainly).

The second problem is the extensive analysis
required. The construction system can use the front-end
output in the domain to first find the outermost-level task
object declarations and then their task type declarations
(and all nested task type declarations). For each of these
task types the use of library package data could be noted,
using inter-section references. ('Sections' are introduced
below.) Hence the data shared between particular tasks could
be determined. However, tasks created from un-nested task
type declarations by the outermost-level task would also
need to be considered. References made to library package
data by these task types would need to be included, which
could require all object declarations to be examined.
Composite types would need to be related to the types of
their components (in case a component is a task type) and so
on, using the symbol tables in the domain.

We thus recommend that shared data accessed by
disparate processors should not be supported; i.e. that a
virtual node should only map onto processors of similar
types. The complexity of doing otherwise is not justified by
the potential gain in flexibility.

6.7.4 Routing of rendezvous communication

Where one task calls an entry of another task,
parameter values and other rendezvous information must be
transmitted between the corresponding parts of the run-time
system.

Cases where the two tasks execute on the same
processor and cases where the processor of the called task
can address the memories containing the objects referenced
by the rendezvous parameters are straightforward, and not
considered here.

a) Direct routing

The simplest case involving routing is where there is a direct physical link between two processors; i.e. a shared memory or a communications line.

The run-time system for each processor needs to know which tasks running on other processors it is possible to communicate with, and what method is needed. This must be decided at run-time where there are dynamically allocated tasks or task access objects.

When a task is dynamically created there will in general be a set of eligible processors for it, one of which will be selected by the run-time system of the parent task. The task descriptor (the contents of a task object or task access object) must therefore identify the processor as well as containing some identification local to the processor kernel that created the task. Thus the run-time system for a calling task will know which processor kernel is responsible for the called task, even with dynamic allocation.

The construction system will build a table for each processor kernel specifying which processors are directly connected and the method of communication for each.

Both parts of the run-time system need buffering space for local copies of the objects referenced by the rendezvous parameters where these cannot be placed on the stack of the called task. This occurs for example when the called task has not yet executed the accept but the initial request from the calling run-time system contains parameters. This space must be dynamically acquired and released because of the arbitrarily-large amount of information that can be transmitted and the arbitrary number of callers.

In general, transmitting information in each direction will require several operations, to conform to a communications protocol on a line, to avoid monopolising a bus, etc. Also if a part of the run-time system supports several tasks it will need to conduct several rendezvous at one time, observing the higher of the priorities (if any) of

the calling and called tasks, as defined by Ada. Only
dealing with one rendezvous at a time would delay higher-
priority tasks that start rendezvous later.

The above has assumed contention for a single
physical link between several concurrent rendezvous, with
task priority determining which rendezvous receives service
at any time. In some application systems tasks might have to
be remote from each other to respond rapidly to local events
but might need fast rendezvous between them. The system
designer might introduce two or more physical links (or
logical channels multiplexed onto one physical link) between
processors. He will specify at allocation-time which tasks
can use which links. Indeed a link might be dedicated to a
pair of tasks. The construction system should allow such
specification and check that the tasks are allocated at each
end of the links allocated to them. Run-time re-allocation
of links might be provided to cope with the failure of a
link.

b) Indirect routing

If the run-time system provides communication
between processors that are not directly linked physically
(i.e. two or more physical links in series must be used) it
must provide a general routing capability for rendezvous
information and other inter-processor traffic. As indicated
above, if nested tasks are not restricted to execution on
the processor of the parent, the need for indirect routing
could arise even where the processors of the two ultimate
ancestor tasks are directly connected. (Or conversely, if
only direct routing is provided there is an extra constraint
on the allocation of nested tasks such that all the
processors of the calling tasks are directly connected.
These calling tasks will be the parent and some of the other
tasks created by the parent.) Also the initial load of the
software into the target before execution starts might need
indirect routing to reduce requirements for local ROM, disc
or tape to hold memory images.

So there is a strong case for the run-time system
to provide a general inter-processor routing service.

Thus the connection table above needs to be
extended to include:
- for each pair of processors, which connection path
  to use, i.e. which series of direct links;
- for each processor, a list of its direct links and
  the communication method to be used for each.

Each routing part of the run-time system must
handle rendezvous information acting just as a communication
agent, without being aware of the significance of the
contents of each transmission.

The provision of indirect communication also
introduces the possibility that there is more than one
possible route between two tasks in rendezvous or, more
generally, between any two points in the route. A variety
of methods of communication become available, such as:
- the route between two tasks can be fixed at
  allocation-time by the user or by the construction
  system;
- the same but with the route decided at the start
  of each rendezvous, perhaps using allocation-time
  specification as the default when no failure has
  occurred;
- the preceding, with the ability to change routes
  during a rendezvous if a failure occurs;
- choosing a route for each individual block of
  rendezvous information;
- multiple transmission of each rendezvous block via
  different routes until acknowledgement is
  received.

The inter-processor communications part of the
run-time system is distinct from the rest of the run-time
system. Its complexity is therefore determined by a trade-
off between size of communication software, elapsed time to
complete a typical rendezvous, buffer space needed to handle
blocks of rendezvous information, protection against
hardware failure, etc.

6.7.5 Generation of the run-time system

a) General structure of the run-time system

It is assumed that the run-time system will consist of a kernel for each processor. Each kernel will handle events local to its processor, such as rendezvous between tasks that are executed by the processor. Processor kernels will cooperate (or compete) for resources needed by more than one kernel, such as heap partitions, communication facilities, shared-memory for rendezvous parameter-passing, and allocation of tasks. This decentralised model is the most suitable for a distributed target.

b) Implementation language

One special feature of distributed targets is the possibility of a mixture of types of hardware (principally processor-MMU combinations). Therefore the run-time system should be written as far as possible in a high-level machine-independent language, preferably a subset of Ada. Obviously, if Ada is used, care must be taken to avoid recursion caused by a part of the run-time system using the facility that it implements.

Any machine-code inserts should be selected by a macro facility or Ada library package facility.

Thus one copy of the run-time system source, with versions only of machine-code inserts, can be used to set up reference domains containing the run-time system routines compiled for a given type of processor.

c) Configuration of the run-time system

When the user (or construction system) has allocated the user-written software to the target configuration the construction system can then determine the requirements for each processor kernel:

- which outermost-level tasks the kernel must support;
- for each type of nested task, which processors are eligible to run tasks of the type;

- which physical heap partitions are used by the
  tasks supported by the kernel and which of these
  are shared with other processor kernels;
- which other processors are connected to this one
  and for each of these what communication path
  should be used, and hence what communication
  software is needed;
- what subset of the run-time system facilities is
  needed to support the allocated tasks and
  communication software.

To discuss the fourth point, the communications
software should be written in Ada. It needs to be configured
for the particular hardware, to reference particular
physical addresses and so on. The communications software
for a particular type of communication link (e.g. a specific
protocol for an RS232 line) should be defined as a generic
package. This can then be instantiated using parameter
values from the configuration information.

This instantiation might be done by the user, who
would also decide which instantiations of communications
software to include. However it should be possible for a
construction system tool to decide from the configuration
information which communications software is needed, i.e.
which packages and which instantiations. It could then
generate the Ada source of each instantiation using the
configuration information; this would require the tool to
know what generic parameters each communications software
package has. The relevant generic package could then be
acquired (logically copied) from a reference domain and the
instantiation could then be compiled and included in the
link.

Inclusion of only the necessary run-time system
functions can be easily achieved if the run-time system is
well structured into sections and the linker has a facility
for selective inclusion of sections, i.e. inclusion only of
sections referenced directly or indirectly by some section
already included. This will enable it to select only those
run-time system sections needed to satisfy the run-time

system calls of the user-written code and the communications software, the run-time system sections referenced by these sections and so on.

If the run-time system is written in a high-level language other than Ada it must be processed into the same linker format as produced by the Ada compilers.

Depending on the processor, the run-time system (or some interface part) might have to be directly linked to the user-written software or it could be separate, entered by some form of supervisor-call instruction.

6.7.6 <u>Elaboration of library units</u>

This discussion assumes that loading of the application system software onto the target is complete before elaboration starts, although these stages could be overlapped.

The library units of an Ada program are those quoted in <u>with</u> clauses by the main subprogram and its sub-units, those quoted by these library units and their sub-units and so on. Ada defines rules for the order in which these are elaborated at run-time before entry to the main subprogram. The programmer can add ordering constraints explicitly by ELABORATE pragmas. Any order that satisfies these constraints is allowed. Elaboration of a library subprogram will typically be a null action but elaboration of a library package could involve the allocation of space for access objects and initialisation of data, including execution of the body of the package. Ordering is necessary because initialisation might involve a call of code in another library unit or use of package data.

In a single-processor target this elaboration will be performed serially. It could also be done serially by one processor in a multiple-processor single-shared-memory target, given suitable addressability. With a distributed target it is necessary for several processors to cooperate in elaboration, observing the order determined by the construction system. This means that there will be several processors each of which has elaboration steps to perform.

Each step must await completion of zero or more elaboration
steps by other processors.

The simplest solution would be central software to
control elaboration, running on one processor. Each
elaboration step would only be done when the central
software sends a message to initiate it. Completion of the
step would be reported back via another message. The run-
time system would provide general inter-processor routing.

A decentralised solution is more suited to a
distributed target. It will only use inter-processor links
where these must be present to support use of the elaborated
software. It is also more efficient because it allows
parallel elaboration.

In this solution when a step is complete the
processor that executed the step must inform each processor
awaiting this completion. So the construction system will
not define an overall order but will supply an order for
each processor, with a set of conditions to be fulfilled
before each step is started and a list of processors to be
informed of completion. Where there is more than one legal
order, the set of orders should be chosen to minimise
interprocessor communication, particularly between remote
processors.

The construction system must determine which
processor will perform each elaboration step. The processor
must be able to address the code to be executed and the
static data structures and heap partitions involved. Also,
the outermost-level tasks will have been allocated to
particular processors, so the run-time system of the
processor that executes a step that involves the creation of
such a task must be able to communicate with the run-time
system of the allocated processor. If the run-time system
does not provide a general routing service, the user will
not have total freedom of where to allocate the outermost-
level tasks.

6.7.7 Linking user-written application system software

a) Sections

Before discussing linking it is necessary to consider what is the elementary chunk of software. It is not the compilation unit, since for example a library package might contain code and data, which need different treatment. Even the code might need to be split up under user control. The user might wish to split up some procedures in a library package so that the construction system will selectively include only those procedures referenced by the program, not all the code of the compilation unit. In this same example the body of a library package might include initialisation code that is executed once only as part of elaboration on start-up of the program, and is then not needed. The user might be able to exploit this, perhaps by placing the code in a separate physical-space or address-space overlay.

For these reasons it is necessary to introduce the concept of a section which is an indivisible chunk of code or data. The compilation of each compilation unit in general produces more than one section. The linker operates on sections. The user will need the ability to define the start of sections by use of pragmas in the Ada source.

Sections should be named. This allows the linker to (logically) combine sections of the same name into bigger sections. It also allows the user to specify how particular sections are to be allocated.

The user could employ this user-specified sectioning to logically separate out the code of task bodies from any surrounding code in a compilation unit. Alternatively the task body can be declared to be separate and hence form one or more compilation units.

It will be recorded for what type of processor each section was compiled.

b) Scope of linking

Note that 'linking' means combining the output of compilation units processed by the Ada compiler. The functions performed in linking are:

- to tie up references between sections in different
  compilation units;
- to complete the Ada translation that cannot be
  done by the Ada compiler because it only sees
  parts of the program (e.g. determining a legal
  elaboration order for library units, allocating
  unique exception numbers);
- to physically combine compiler output (reducing
  the number of files);
- to logically combine input sections of the same
  name.

Thus linking does not include building binary
images nor assigning addresses. The output of the linker is
a series of directives to the builder.

c) Linking

The whole Ada program must be linked. Code
sections will have been compiled for a particular type of
processor. The linker must ensure that a reference to a
code section is satisfied by the version for the appropriate
type of processor.

Partial linking will be useful, given the
possibility of re-allocation or re-configuration, to avoid
complete re-linking of all the compilation units in the
program when this occurs. Useful partial links might be:

- the code of a task type, compiled for a given type
  of processor;
- the link of a VN's code and data.

It should be noted that sections of different
names in a partial link will still be logically separate,
capable of being individually allocated to memories.

Also there will be only one copy of a section in a
link, regardless of how many instances of the section will
be allocated. For example code might be replicated during
allocation, if one copy could not be addressed by all tasks
that use it, or to reduce bus traffic. Conversely, if two
tasks running on the same type of processor have sections in
common, only one instance of the section might be allocated
if addressing and performance constraints allow.

6.7.8 Code replication

The potential for code sharing between tasks can arise via:

- several tasks of one type;
- use of a library package or library subprogram by more than one task;
- nested task type declarations.

In a single memory system, code sharing is a useful optimisation with few disadvantages. In a distributed system the extent of code-sharing is determined by a compromise between, on one hand, the saving of physical memory and, on the other, the addressability constraints imposed on the hardware configuration and the contention when several processors use one bus to access a shared copy of a piece of code. The trend will be to replicate code for performance reasons and to avoid restrictions on the flexibility of target configurations.

Code replication is not a problem, given the form of linker output assumed above. One section can be used by the builder to produce several instances. Replication does introduce the need for decisions:

- on which sections to replicate and where to allocate them;
- for a task whose processor can address more than one instance of a section, which section to map.

It is difficult for the construction system to decide to replicate for performance reasons. It could have simple rules about the number of processors that can share one copy of code in a multi-ported memory or that can use one bus to share one copy of the code but only the user knows the frequency with which the code will be executed.

However if replication for performance is specified by the user, the construction system can decide on replication needed because of addressability and limitations on the sizes of shared memories. The construction system will decide on replication after (if user-specified) or during (if done by the construction system) the allocation of outermost-level tasks to processors. The construction

system can determine which code sections are shared in one
or more of the three ways above. If a code section is to be
replicated the construction system can determine what other
sections it references and hence replicate them, and so on.
The construction system should certainly decide which
instance of a section to use when more than one is eligible.

6.7.9 Symbolic debugging

Symbolic debugging is especially important in Ada,
with its tasking and non-deterministic control structures,
coupled with the fact that the application system is a
single program. With Ada on a distributed target, debugging
becomes harder because the run-time system is decentralised
and the parallelism becomes more genuine. It will be harder
for the tester to obtain an overall picture of what is
happening in the system because it will not be possible
precisely to correlate events in different parts of the
target. It is also more difficult to synchronise the
suspension of the entire application system when the tester
requires it or when a breakpoint is executed by one of the
processors.

Thus one approach to the design of the debugging
system is for the tester to observe only a local part of the
target, for example to monitor a processor kernel or the
kernels for the processors on a given bus.

This might be good enough if the tasks executing
on this processor (or processors) have a simple monitorable
interface with the rest of the application system, i.e. via
rendezvous, which is handled by the run-time system, rather
than via shared memory, which is not. A VN has only
rendezvous interfaces but its tasks could be distributed
over a set of processors not on one bus. This will require
testing to be considered in the design of task interfaces.
Of course, it is always necessary to design an application
system so that it can be tested satisfactorily.

If the debugging approach is to attempt to monitor
the entire application system it is not sufficient to add a
debugging monitor to each processor kernel. No attempt at

simultaneity can be made. Also debug commands and responses
will need to be routed through inter-processor links, with
higher priority than other traffic. This would require the
run-time system to have a general routing capability. It
would also be useless for tests where communication paths
are failed deliberately to examine the application system
response. It is assumed that the tester operates via a
single terminal rather than using several terminals which
might be physically distant.

Therefore a set of debugging monitors would be
needed, one for each bus, with its own processor and memory.
These monitors would need dedicated links for communication
between them and with the host. These links would be
additional to the application system hardware.

If the entire application system is to be frozen
when some significant event has occurred this will have to
be done by hardware, for example to acquire each bus for the
local monitor processor as soon as possible after the
request, thus halting all application system processors and
DMA devices connected to the bus.

The debugging support software on the target must
be generated largely automatically, as for the normal run-
time system. Thus it should be written in Ada in the form
of generic packages and tailored by instantiation like the
communications software.

6.7.10 Automation
The question of the degree of automation of the
construction system has been touched on already. There are
two extreme approaches:
- The user controls individual construction system
  tools. Probably the construction system performs
  some form of consistency checking during linking
  and allocation.
- The construction system has a master tool which
  employs individual tools like the compiler and
  linker.

The degree of automation of the construction
system is not directly relevant to the distribution of the
application system, but it is more important compared to
non-distributed systems because of:
- the objective of coping conveniently with reconfiguration and/or re-allocation;
- the greater difficulty in making an allocation
  that satisfies constraints such as addressability;
- keeping track of versions of code compiled for
  different types of processor.

A fully automated approach would require the
application system writer to specify the configuration and
allocation information before any compilation could occur.
(Versions of STANDARD and SYSTEM have to be selected before
the compiler front-end can be used on the Ada source.)
Possibly, sufficient outline information could be supplied,
with more details later in the construction process.

Apses should ease automation by providing good
facilities for one tool to control others and by providing a
powerful database.

7

Implications for the Apse toolset

7.1 INTRODUCTION

Current Apse projects concern Mapses, "minimal" Apses. At the level of discussion here the Mapse projects mentioned in chapter 4 present similar problems; we will not distinguish between them.

It is evident, from the analysis in chapter 6, that a construction system for distributed hardware differs substantially from those proposed in existing Mapse designs. This chapter identifies which tools envisaged for Mapses could be used with little or no modification and discusses the implications for the tool support environment, the Kapse.

Sections 7.2 to 7.7 consider the implications for the Ada compilation domain (library file), for the principal Mapse tools (the compiler, the linker, the builder, and the symbolic debugger), and for the run-time system.

Subsequent sections consider checking for adherence to the virtual node (VN) restrictions , the tool structure of the construction system, and the information that must be supplied by the user.

7.2 THE COMPILATION DOMAIN, OR LIBRARY FILE

This is the structure used to store compiler output, including any intermediate forms such as Diana trees, as well as partial links. (The Ada separate compilation rules require compiler output to be stored in a special place, manipulable only by trusted tools.) The domain is affected by:

(i) multiple versions of the specification and body of packages STANDARD and SYSTEM;

(ii) the use of several compilers (for different processor types) on one compilation unit.

Where the domain is implemented in terms of the Kapse database it should be straightforward to extend it to cope with multiple versions. It should also be possible to arrange that any particular execution of the compiler front-end or back-end operates in the context of a particular version, set by some controlling tool.

7.3 <u>THE COMPILER</u>

The structure of the compilers needs to be considered. To simplify our discussion, we have referred to different compilers for each target processor type. In practice there will be a family of compilers; there will typically be a target independent "front-end", and target dependent "back-ends". The compiler controller will invoke the front-end, using appropriate versions of packages SYSTEM and STANDARD, and then invoke the appropriate back-end. Intermediate representations will be stored in the domain.

Some actions arising from distribution must be performed by the compiler, or related tools, because the object code generated from the user-written source is affected:

(i) adding run-time type information to the code generated from task object or task access object declarations, in order that the run-time system can determine which processors are eligible to run each task;

(ii) processing heap partition name pragmas for access types; adding details of the logical partition to the code generated from access object declarations, for use by the run-time system;

(iii) adding details of heap partitions to the set of memories used by the parameters of a rendezvous (to cope with composite types involving access types);

(iv) adding run-time parameter type information to
entry calls, for value representation conversion
where the processors of the calling and called
tasks are of different types;

(v) acting on generalised representation clauses
(lists of processor types) for shared data
accessed by more than one type of processor.

Action (ii) will probably require modification to
the compiler front-end.

Action (v) requires the back-end to understand and
act on such generalised representation clauses.

Action (i), the second part of (ii), and actions
(iii) and (iv) could in principle be done by a separate
tool. This would use the symbol table and intermediate code
created by the front-end to manipulate the input or output
of the back-end to add the appropriate information. However
compilation would be more efficient if these actions were
incorporated in the back-end.

7.4 THE LINKER

The actions that affect the generated program and
for which the linker is responsible are:

(i) establishing a set of initial elaboration steps
for a number of processors, themselves selected
primarily by addressability of the code to be
executed and data to be updated;

(ii) handling versions for different processor types of
the code of a compilation unit; also ensuring that
linked code sections are for the same type of
processor;

(iii) converting the numbering of task and rendezvous
parameter object types from a scheme local to a
compilation unit to one that covers the whole
program.

Thus the linker will need to be modified, but only
in a straightforward way. A similar action to that in (iii)
is already needed for exception numbering.

Action (i) depends on allocation information.
Whether this is available at link-time depends on the degree
of automation. So the determination of the initial
elaboration order might have to be removed from the linker
and be done by a separate tool after allocation.

7.5 THE BUILDER

This takes the output from the linker and builds a
program image. Conventionally, linking and building is done
by one tool, but linking is largely target-independent
whereas building is heavily target-dependent so Mapses
separate these functions into distinct tools (or sub-tools
of one tool).

The builder for distributed hardware will be new.
Its input and functions are considered in section 7.10
below; much can be learned from the MML Distributed Program
Builder. The builder will have a master tool which performs
allocation and checking of allocation constraints. The code
of this master tool will be largely target independent and
hence will be written once only.

There is probably scope for the master tool to use
Mapse builders to construct each memory image, selecting the
appropriate builder(s) for the types of processor that will
use the memory. Some modification to Mapse builders will be
necessary to allow this.

7.6 THE SYMBOLIC DEBUGGER

Symbolic debuggers have target-independent parts
and target-dependent parts. The target-dependent parts will
be split between the host and the target (if separate); the
target-resident part will monitor breakpoints, examine and
change target locations, and communicate with the host. The
larger target-independent parts, running on the host,
interact with the user and access the domain and other
program construction information; these parts should be
usable for distributed targets.

However current Mapse debugger designs incorporate
single shared memory assumptions, such as:

- there is only one copy of the code of a task type;
- there is a centralised run-time system which can immediately halt the entire program (system) when a task executes a breakpoint.

Work will be needed to remove any such assumptions. The second one is fundamental to the debugging philosophy and its removal could require significant redesign.

7.7 THE RUN-TIME SYSTEM

It is evident from efficiency considerations that the run-time system for distributed hardware will have to be designed afresh. An approach which attempts to re-use existing run-time system designs and code by adding a virtual machine environment to these existing systems would introduce unacceptable time overheads. However, parts of the run-time system for distributed hardware will be the same, or nearly the same, as for existing run-time system designs (e.g. heap management, exception handling, much of task creation). Thus these parts of the design of existing run-time systems and, to some extent, the Ada source, can be re-used.

7.8 PROGRAM CHECKING

The program must be checked to ensure adherence to the VN restrictions. This involves:

(i) checking for non-rendezvous communication between VNs (i.e. shared data or code);

(ii) determining the possible references between logical heap partitions (from types that include access types), and checking for references between physical partitions after allocation;

(iii) noting the tasks where the conditional entry call facility has been used, and reporting when there is no sufficiently fast route (shared memory, dedicated line) between the processors to which the tasks are allocated;

(iv) noting the use (direct or indirect) of access
types in rendezvous, checking that calling and
called tasks are in the same VN, and checking that
the processors of the calling and called tasks can
both address the memory containing the relevant
physical heap partitions.

These checks should be performed by a separate
tool, using allocation information and operating on
information in the domain such as symbol tables and the
intermediate code. (Only check (i) can be completed before
allocation.)

Keeping these checking functions separate also
allows convenient re-checking when allocation or the
composition of VNs is changed.

However, such checking is essential; there is no
question of relying on the user to run the checking tool.
Instead it will be incorporated as a sub-tool of the tools
that handle allocation or re-specification of the
composition of VNs.

7.9 OVERALL STRUCTURE OF THE CONSTRUCTION SYSTEM

Figure 7.1 shows a possible outline structure.
Tools envisaged in existing Mapse designs are given names
including the word 'Mapse'.

In the arrangement shown the user is responsible
for deciding for which processor types a given Ada
compilation unit should be processed.

A more automated construction system than that
shown in Figure 7.1 would first accept target configuration
information and then allocation instructions. It would then
automatically run appropriate compilers on each compilation
unit submitted to it. Change of the configuration or
allocation information would lead to automatic recompilation of previously-submitted compilation units as
required. (This could use their abstract syntax tree
representation, generated by the front-end and stored in the
domain.) Such a construction system would use many of the
same tools as the less automated system shown.

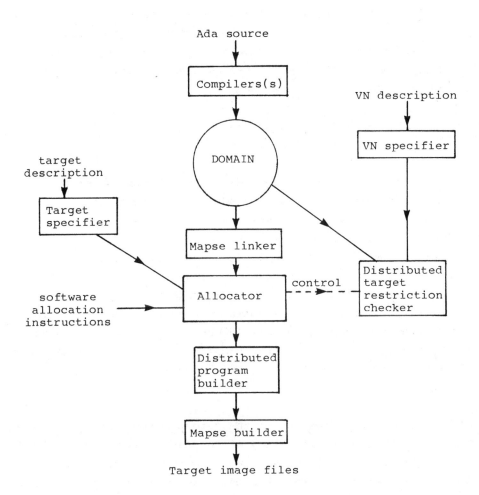

Figure 7.1 A Possible Structure for the Construction System.

7.10 <u>INFORMATION REQUIRED FROM THE USER</u>

This section summarises the information that must be supplied to the construction system. Only the information content is considered, not the actual syntax.

A construction system that is not fully automatic will need more detailed allocation instructions.

The user must be able to control the allocation of outermost-level tasks to processors. A mechanism is also needed to control this for nested tasks to ensure performance criteria are met.

7.10.1 <u>Specification of VNs</u>
a) Specification

The user will need to say to which VN each task belongs. This merely requires a list of task names for each named VN. Nested tasks need not be included; they will be in the same VN as the task in which they are declared.

This information is used to check whether non-rendezvous communication between any two tasks is allowed.
b) Impact of re-specification

If the composition of VNs is re-specified the check for non-rendezvous communication between VNs must be re-applied. This is one reason why the checker tool above should not be a part of the compiler. Where a task has been moved between VNs it will often be possible to avoid recompilation.

7.10.2 <u>Specification of the target configuration</u>

The configuration of the target hardware should not be part of the Ada source, to allow redistribution without source program changes. The input will be processed and checked by a special construction system tool.

The configuration information has two phases:
- description of the hardware content of the target;
- description of the composition of hardware nodes (HNs).

The latter can be re-specified for the same configuration.

It is not always clear what information must be 'built-in' to the construction system tools rather than being parameterised in the configuration information. Knowledge of the instruction set of a processor must be built into a compiler back-end for that processor. On the other hand it is not obvious that the construction system tools have to be specialised to particular schemes of memory-mapping. It is clearly preferable that run-time definition of the various schemes used by different types of hardware can be used.

The information required from the user about the hardware configuration is as follows:

For each memory bank:
- a name for the memory;
- the types of access allowed (e.g. ROM or RAM);
- memory-unit size (e.g. 16-bit);
- total size of memory (in memory units);
- error detection and error correction attributes.

For each processor (including its memory mapping, if any):
- a name;
- the type of the processor (e.g. Motorola 68000);
- options such as floating-point units;
- the structure of virtual addresses (e.g N-bit address space number and M-bit offset in memory units within address space); this might well need to be more complicated, depending on the memory-mapping schemes possible with the types of hardware with which the construction system can cope;
- protection modes available for an address space (e.g read-only, execute-only, read-write).

The structure of addresses indicates the total addressing capability and the granularity of the mapping. Processors without mapping are a degenerate case.

Some processor types will not include floating-point instructions but will have an optional separate floating-point unit available. The compiler back-end should

use the configuration information to see if hardware
floating-point is available or if software routines must be
used instead. Floating-point units will logically be part of
the associated processor (i.e. an extension to the
instruction set) and hence only their presence needs to be
recorded.

For each bus:
- a name for the bus;
- the name and physical start address of each memory
  bank attached to the bus;
- the name of each processor attached to the bus;
- for each inter-HN connection, its name, the type
  of link (e.g. RS232 link, parallel link, network),
  and details that are specific to the type of link
  (e.g. physical addresses, protocol, etc). The
  information required here depends on whether the
  user or the construction system is configuring the
  inter-processor communication software.

Details of the physical connections between HNs
can be extracted from the information above. Some of these
connections might provide more than one logical channel. If
so, the configuration information should specify how many
channels are available in a connection.

There might be more than one physical connection
between a pair of HNs. If so it would be useful if the
configuration information indicated the approximate
effective throughput of the logical channels (e.g. bits per
second, taking the overhead of the protocol into account).
An automated system could ensure that the higher-priority
tasks were allocated to the higher-speed routes.

The user must also specify the physical
composition of each hardware node. HNs consist of
processors, memories, buses and connections; just a list of
names is needed for each HN.

VNs depend on the HNs onto which they are mapped,
and the HNs depend on the components of the hardware
configuration. With Apse database facilities it should be
easy to represent VNs, HNs and hardware components as

database objects and hence determine the VNs affected by HN
or configuration re-specification.

7.10.3 Specification of the software allocation

The user must specify how the software is to be
allocated to the different parts of the target. He might
also wish to specify allocation constraints that the
construction system should check are met in the given
configuration and allocation.

These instructions will be provided in some simple
specification language. They will be processed and checked
by a special construction system tool, which will also have
as input the processed configuration information.

a) Allocation instructions

In a fully automated system the user would need
only specify for each VN which HN it is mapped onto, with
guidance on the allocation of outermost-level tasks to
processors. The construction system would then decide on
code replication and allocation of code, data, and channels.

For a simpler construction system the user will
need to allocate instances of sections of code and data to
memories and tasks to processors.

For each VN, the user would have to specify the
allocation of:

   (i) outermost-level tasks to processors;

  (ii) stack space to be used by a given processor kernel
      to a memory;

 (iii) mapping of logical heap partitions to physical
      heap partitions, and the allocation of space for
      each physical partition to a memory;

  (iv) instances of sections of code to memories,
      including the run-time system code sections;
      several instances of code sections can be
      allocated;

(v) one instance of each static data section to a
   memory;

As noted earlier, there might be more than one
logical channel between HNs, because of more than one
physical connection and/or channels multiplexed onto a
connection. The user will need to be able to allocate:

(vi) logical channels to outermost-level tasks, to
     arrange that high-priority tasks get fast channels
     and, in particular, reduced competition for these
     channels from other tasks.

b) Allocation constraints

There are some implicit constraints and some the
user can or must specify.

Implicit constraints

(i) The processor to which a task is allocated must be
    able to address all the code the task could
    execute and all the data it could directly access
    (static data, stacks of parent tasks, heap). This
    also applies to the part of the run-time system
    that supports the task.

(ii) The connection of interrupt locations to entries
     of tasks must be checked against the allocation of
     tasks to processors.

(iii) Code and data assigned to particular addresses via
      representation clauses must be checked against the
      allocation of tasks to processors.

(iv) The tasks allocated to a logical channel must be
     allocated to the processors connected by the
     channel.

(v) Where the construction system can determine that
    rendezvous between two tasks involves access
    objects the processors of the calling and called
    tasks must both be able to address the memory
    containing the physical heap partition for each
    access type.

(vi) Where the construction system can determine that
conditional entry calls are made between two
tasks, the processors of the tasks must share
memory or the tasks must have a dedicated channel
allocated to them.

(vii) If the run-time system only provides communication
between directly-connected processors, the
allocation of outermost-level tasks to processors
is constrained (as is that of nested tasks).

Check (ii) is straightforward since the 'interrupt
location' that is part of the representation clause will
include the name of the processor.

Check (iii) requires that the address types in the
versions of package SYSTEM must include a field for the name
of the processor.

User-defined constraints

The user must define the pairs of tasks where the
offline analysis of the construction system for points (v)
and (vi) cannot detect access objects in rendezvous or the
use of conditional entry calls. Primarily this is when an
entry call is made via a task access object.

The user might also wish to specify the
communication routes between indirectly-connected
processors.

7.11 SUMMARY

It will not be possible to use current Mapse tools
without change in a construction system for distributed
hardware. However the modifications required for the
compiler and linker are small. The symbolic debugger is
likely to be extensively affected by the need to deal with a
decentralised run-time system. Mapse builders can probably
be used, with some modification, as part of the builder for
distributed hardware.

Only part of the design, and possibly some of the
Ada source, of existing run-time systems will be re-usable
for the run-time system for distributed hardware.

Most of the checking actions can be handled by
separate tools, using the wealth of information capable of
being generated by Ada compilers and stored in the domain.
Some transformation actions could be done by separate tools,
at a cost of reduced efficiency.

New tools are needed:

- to accept, modify and display specifications of
  VNs, configuration and allocation, and to
  determine the effect of re-specification;
- to generate the run-time system, including
  tailoring the communications software, generating
  the source of routines to convert the
  representation of rendezvous parameter values,
  producing data structures describing the
  configuration local to a processor, determining
  the eligible processors for nested tasks and
  recording this in a data structure, and so on;
- to control the building of memory images from
  input links and VN, configuration and allocation
  information.

8
Reliability and extensibility

8.1 INTRODUCTION

Many computer systems are required to continue
execution in the face of the most serious adversity.
Multiprocessor systems may even be required to continue
execution with degraded performance after failure of a
considerable proportion of the hardware. The problems
involved with coping with such situations are considered
here in the context of multiprocessor systems written in
Ada.

Both hardware and software can cause abnormal
situations to arise and so we will differentiate between
these by calling software problems errors and hardware
failures faults.

Ada provides exceptions for handling errors and
unexpected situations but other mechanisms are required for
some situations particularly relating to the detection and
recovery from abnormal situations.

8.2 REQUIREMENTS

In order to provide reliability and extensibility
a distributed multiprocessor computer system must cope with
unexpected faults and errors, and with intentional physical
and functional changes. Although similar, these
requirements differ because of the characteristics of the
two types of disturbance. Faults may have been foreseen but
are not desired or controlled. They may occur in any
combination at unpredictable times and may require quick
recovery, particularly in real-time embedded systems. In
comparison, physical and functional changes are planned and

fully controlled by an external operator and may take place
over longer timescales.

8.2.1 Hardware fault tolerance

Hardware faults vary in scale and duration, from
transient memory faults to the failure of multiprocessor
nodes. Furthermore, the reliability requirements of each
application may be different, ranging from a need for
complete reliability for short periods, as in flight
control, to continued service with acceptable degradation in
commercial environments. Consequently, a wide variety of
techniques for fault avoidance and fault tolerance have been
developed and reported in the literature. An extensive
survey of hardware faults, reliability requirements and a
range of appropriate recovery and protection measures is
given in Wensley et al (1974). See also Hopkins (1980) and
Rennels (1980).

Fault avoidance techniques applied in the design
phase can reduce the probability of faults but never
eradicate them. Consequently there is a need to tolerate
hardware faults during run-time so as to continue execution
and preserve data integrity. Achieving fault tolerance
requires the application of a strategy comprising error
detection, damage confinement and assessment, error
recovery, fault treatment and continued service stages
(Anderson & Lee 1981).

Distributed multiprocessor computer systems offer
both opportunities and problems for fault tolerance. They
must emulate the fault tolerance of uniprocessor systems but
are also capable of surviving larger scale faults such as
the loss of a processor. This requires more extensive
recovery mechanisms, bearing in mind that the failure of a
processor, for example, may result in the loss of many tasks
and much data and state information.

Recovery from faults may be based on the Apse, for
example by reloading and restarting lost processes, but in
many applications an Apse may not be available or real-time
demands will not permit its use. In these circumstances

responsibility for fault tolerance must reside in the
hardware, the run-time system and the Ada application
program. Ideally the run-time support software should hide
faults and subsequent recovery from the applications program
but this is not always possible. Some faults, such as the
failure of entire hardware nodes containing multiple
processors or the fragmentation of a distributed system into
isolated sub-systems following communication network
failure, are too severe to hide. The Ada applications
program designer must be aware of potentially severe faults
and structure the program accordingly. An example of
distributed software organisation that tolerates major
faults by distributing and replicating critical functions
and data, and by decentralising control is given in Hull et
al. (1983).

8.2.2 Software error tolerance

Software errors may be the result of residual
design faults. Unlike hardware, software is not subject to
the effects of decay (Randell 1975). Ada was designed to
reduce residual design errors by encouraging highly modular
and structured software design through the use of functional
decomposition, information hiding and strong type checking.
Nevertheless software errors will occur in Ada programs;
indeed it is argued by Hoare (1981) that they are made more
likely by the complexity of Ada.

As with faults, errors must be tolerated during
run-time. The main requirements are similar, namely to
continue execution, to preserve data integrity and to
prevent the propagation of erroneous results, and will need
the application of a similar fault tolerance strategy.

Two main techniques have been developed for
software error tolerance, where the errors are assumed to
arise from design mistakes: recovery blocks (Randell 1975)
and N-Version programming (Chen & Avizienis 1978). These
techniques are concerned with sequential programs and so are
not affected by the organisation of distributed Ada programs
as communicating sequential processes, except by the

potential for concurrent execution of N-Version alternative
algorithms. A new requirement is for techniques to deal
with residual design faults in the high-level structure of
Ada programs, for example in the organisation and use of
inter-task communication. Virtual nodes offer an approach
based on the restriction of inter-node communication and the
prevention of error propagation. It must be possible at
least to redirect inter-task communication dynamically to
implement recovery. Dynamic creation or migration of
virtual nodes will be needed for more flexible recovery
schemes.

8.2.3 Physical extensibility

Physical extensibility is concerned with changing
the physical configuration of a distributed multiprocessor
computer system without disturbing the Ada application
program being executed. In particular it is not concerned
with changes to the Ada program itself. Typical causes of
physical change are incremental expansion, preventative
maintenance and redistribution of system load. Two
important characteristics are that the changes are made
intentionally and controlled externally.

To redistribute the load, one or more virtual
nodes must be moved. Prior to changing the physical
location of a virtual node the feasibility of the intended
new mapping must be checked with regard to the availability
of needed resources, peripherals and memory, and the
connectivity to communicating virtual node partners.
Following this, the first stage of relocation must be to
halt the virtual node at its original site, not forgetting
the possibility of having to deal with existing rendezvous
associated with the virtual node. Next, the code for the
virtual node must be down loaded to the new location. This
may require recompilation if the source and destination
physical nodes are different machines. Unaffected virtual
nodes may need to be relinked to the relocated virtual node,
for example via new virtual channels, perhaps requiring the
generation of novel communication paths. Finally the

relocated virtual node must be restarted. A cold start will
lead to the loss of process data and state information while
a warm start requires the transfer of that data and state
(including stack and heap data) to the new location, again
with possible translation to cope with the existence of
different machines.

The primary requirement for physical extensibility
is therefore the availability of an Apse containing the
appropriate tools. The Apse may be physically separate or
it may be a part of the distributed system as in the Conic
system (Kramer et al. 1983) developed to support physical
extensibility with cold start.

8.2.4 Functional extensibility

As with physical extensibility, functional
extensibility is concerned with planned, operator controlled
changes. However, these changes are to the functionality of
the Ada program executing on the distributed computer system
rather than to the hardware of the system. The need for
functional extensibility is to meet the changing demands
placed on the program and is especially important for
systems designed for long term use.

Functional extensibility is concerned with what
the Ada program does rather than how it does it, that is
with specifications rather than with bodies. The
requirement is to make the desired functional changes
without disturbing or recompiling unaffected parts of the
program, without damaging the affected parts and without
compromising type checking.

The main problem deriving from Ada is that of
dependency. Program units that name or use affected units
must be recompiled in order to use the modified versions.
Recompilation can then continue in the correct order as
program units that name recompiled units are themselves
recompiled. There is a requirement to prevent the spread of
recompilation by the use of indirect naming schemes or by
arranging virtual nodes to be independently compiled units
similar to Conic modules (Magee & Kramer 1983).

A second major requirement, addressed in section
8.4.2, is the transfer of process data and state information
to the modified versions of the affected program units so as
to allow these to warm start.

8.3 APPROACHES

In this section some approaches to satisfying the
requirements in section 8.2 are introduced. The approaches
chosen are not exhaustive but are varied. None will satisfy
all the requirements but cover a wide range of possible
techniques. Details of how each approach satisfies the
relevant requirements are given in sections 8.4 and 8.5.

8.3.1 Triple module redundancy

In a triple modular redundant (TMR) system, the
processing systems are triplicated and connected via
synchronisation and voting mechanisms. All processing
systems run identical software and the synchronisation
mechanism ensures that the systems are synchronised with
respect to the input stream. Therefore each system should
produce the same output when working correctly. The voting
mechanism compares outputs and raises a suitable alarm if
differences are detected.

When designing TMR systems, care must be taken
with any non- replicated hardware in the voting and
synchronisation mechanisms. Faults here can cause the whole
system to fail regardless of the state of each of the
processor subsystems. Typically voting is done at the level
of addresses generated and data written in each memory
cycle. Such hardware is simple so it can be designed to
achieve high reliability. The problems in non-replicated
voting and synchronisation mechanisms can be overcome with
the use of replication and periodic testing of the
mechanisms.

The TMR principle can be enhanced in a number of
ways, for example by using more than three processor
systems, by using processor systems with different hardware
and by using different algorithms. As this method is

independent of the language being used, it is not discussed
further.

8.3.2 Recovery Cache

Backward error recovery is a technique in which,
after an unanticipated error is detected, the system is
restored to an earlier state which is believed to be
correct. A recovery cache provides hardware assistance for
backward error recovery using the recovery block technique
described in Horning et al. (1974).

A recovery cache forms part of a basic
processor/memory system. A description of one form of cache
has been given in Lee et al. (1980). In practice it would be
desirable to incorporate such hardware recovery mechanisms
in both the CPU and the memory rather than on the bus. The
cache stores the initial values of any memory locations
whose content is changed during execution of a block. At the
end of the block is an integrity check / acceptance test.
If exit from a recovery block is successful, the cache is
flushed, ready for entry into the next recovery block.
Alternatively, if the check fails, then the previous memory
state can be recovered using the data stored in the cache
and an alternative algorithm is used. Blocks can be nested,
hence the need for "recursion" in the cache.

In Ada, unanticipated failures could also be
indicated by exceptions being raised. When the previous
memory state has been recovered, the section of code can be
repeated using an alternative algorithm and/or hardware.
The first attempt algorithm, alternative algorithm(s) and
the integrity check can be placed inside procedures. These
could be called from a driving program which could also call
routines that control the cache.

8.3.3 Static reconfiguration

A static reconfiguration approach can be used on
multiprocessor systems that do not support dynamic task
creation. The application software is built for one
particular target configuration, but if, at some future

time, the configuration of the target machine changes (e.g.
after a hardware failure) then the application software for
the new configuration is rebuilt on the host machine,
tested, loaded onto the reconfigured target machine and run.

Clearly the static reconfiguration cycle, as
described above, could take considerable time. The method
can be enhanced by building and testing application software
for a number of carefully chosen alternative target
configurations in advance and by loading the code for each
configuration onto the target machine when the system is
built. The configuration currently required to be run on
the target could then be selected either by the operator or
automatically by the run-time system.

8.3.4 Dynamic reconfiguration

The dynamic reconfiguration approach is
characterised by the ability of the application software to
reconfigure itself simply by the activation and the
termination of tasks. Tasks may be terminated by normal
completion, as a result of an unhandled exception or
abortion, or alternatively by the run-time system following
a hardware failure, as if aborted. This last is not strictly
allowed in Ada; a liberal interpretation of the language
definition must be accepted, e.g. as in Inveradi (1982).

The dynamic reconfiguration approach provides the
application programmer with a large amount of flexibility,
all expressible within the program code. For example it is
possible to run three copies of a task on separate
processors and, in effect, simulate TMR. There is, in
addition, the flexibility to use dissimilar processors and
even run different algorithms. However this flexibility is
not achieved without cost. For example, task activation
tends to be a very expensive operation, particularly if
there are routing tables to be updated in the inter-
processor communication system. Also, as the software
configuration changes, unchanged parts may need to be given
the names of new tasks so that communication can continue
and may have to carry out degraded functions to allow the

whole system to continue in a degraded state.

8.4 APPROACHES NOT SPECIFIC TO ADA

This section describes a number of methods that
are not directly relevant to fault tolerance in
multiprocessor systems written in Ada, but that could be
used in conjunction with Ada-specific methods to construct
faster and more reliable methods of recovering from hardware
faults and software errors. The methods apply at different
stages and will have to be used in conjunction with one
another.

The integrity of a system, that is the continuing
correct operation of the system, encompasses the total
system design. Integrity is only achieved by detailed
consideration of all the following aspects:
- error/fault avoidance (at design time)
- error/fault detection (at run-time),
- error/fault confinement (at run-time),
- reporting of the abnormal situation (at run-time),
- recovery from any abnormal situation to some
  acceptable state (at run-time).

8.4.1 Modularity

Modularity is required for error avoidance and for
run-time aspects. It is generally accepted that a modular
approach to writing software assists in the production of
fault free software. In this context Ada assists in the
production of resilient software. It also provides
comprehensive static checking of interfaces and dynamic
error handling in the form of exceptions. However,
exceptions cannot cope with those errors that are not
anticipated by the system designer or that can not be
handled at the application program level. Modularity is a
prerequisite for all the run-time methods suggested for
coping with such errors.

If a system were composed of completely
independent tasks, then the restoration of state of a failed
process would be purely local to that failed process.

However, in practical systems, processes interact with one
another and state changes in one process can be propagated
to another. Failures are expected to be rare events but,
when an error does occur in one of a number of interacting
processes, then errors will tend to propagate through the
system at an exponentially increasing rate. It is therefore
important to structure a system so that a potential error
can be localised as much as possible. Error confinement
requires testing all data across boundaries together with
frequent checkpointing in order to save the state of the
error free system. Checkpointing and testing will contribute
an overhead to the fault free system. A degree of
compromise may often be necessary in order to provide both
acceptable levels of recovery when failures do occur and an
acceptable run-time system performance while the system is
functioning correctly. The design of a system to include
fault tolerance will of course add considerably to its
development cost.

      The static decomposition of an Ada program into
software components is aimed at reducing system complexity.
At run-time, the system possesses a dynamic structure which
reflects the activity of the system. The structure of the
dynamic system is determined by the software components
together with the relationships between them. When
considering reliability, in particular when determining the
possible damage a fault has caused, the information passed
between software components is as important as the control
flow aspects of component structuring (for example, the
existence, deletion and creation of tasks).

      The concept of an _atomic action_ (Lomet 1977)
assists in expressing the dynamic structure of the activity
of a system. An atomic action is an action that must not be
interrupted so there is no flow of information to or from
the rest of the system during the action. It acts on
objects which cannot be simultaneously accessed by other
parts of the system. An atomic action could involve several
tasks since a task executing an atomic action may create
temporary tasks to help it, allowing a number of tasks to

cooperate directly in a shared atomic action such that their overall activity is atomic with respect to all other tasks in the system. Atomic actions can be nested; thus an inner task could itself be an atomic action or contain atomic actions. The system designer specifies which software components must be prevented from interacting, if possible, in order to maintain system integrity. In other words, the designer indicates sequences of atomic operations of a task or a group of sub-tasks, which are to be executed atomically.

By regarding the activity of a system as being composed of certain components, by ignoring their inner details and by considering only the relationships between them, the system is abstractly structured. The importance of atomic actions to the achievement of fault tolerance lies in the framework they provide for error detection and in confining or limiting the possible consequences of a fault. Error confinement can be provided by checkpointing upon entering an atomic action and by detecting a possible error immediately before exit from the atomic action.

Recoverability arises from the indivisibility of atomic actions. As far as the rest of the system is concerned the overall effect of the atomic action is all or nothing, that is either all its objects remain in their initial state or all change to their final state. If a failure should occur during execution of an atomic action, it must be possible either to complete the atomic action (forward error recovery) or to restore all objects to their initial states (backward error recovery).

Forward error recovery is a difficult technique to implement since the precise nature of the fault needs to be known in order that damage assessment and repair can be performed. Backward error recovery is relatively simple since no account need be taken of the nature of the fault involved.

One simple way of implementing the indivisibility property of atomic actions is to enforce atomic actions to run sequentially. This is not desirable since we are

concerned with systems containing a great deal of
concurrency. In order to provide indivisibility in the
presence of concurrency, access to shared objects must be
synchronised so that one atomic action is prevented from
interfering with the intermediate states of another one.

Synchronisation and recovery are likely to be
expensive to implement. It may prove less costly to
implement synchronisation by carefully designing the
structure of the system to minimise synchronisation in the
run-time system. In order to implement the recoverability
property, we need to undo the changes made to objects by
aborted atomic actions. This could prove prohibitively
costly without hardware assistance.

8.4.2 State saving and restoration

An exception handler describes the appropriate
action to be taken if and when an anticipated abnormality
arises. A method is required to complement exception
handling so that unexpected faults can be handled. One
method of coping with such unexpected faults is the recovery
block approach which an erroneous state of the computation
in progress is abandoned and rolled back to a previous state
which is believed to be error free. After the rollback, the
computation is resumed with the hope of avoiding the
offending fault. If, after rollback, a different algorithm
designed to the same specification is used to resume
computation then a degree of tolerance against software
design errors is obtained. If the error detection mechanism
is sufficiently sophisticated to identify a fault as being
due to a transient error, a simple re-try is all that is
necessary to recover from the erroneous state. If, on the
other hand, a hardware fault is permanent or can not be
recognised as a transient fault, reconfiguration of the
hardware may be necessary for recovery to be achieved.
Recovery from an erroneous state can only occur after a
fault has been detected. It will be assumed that hardware
mechanisms exist which signal if a processor is faulty,
perhaps allowing retries to detect transient errors. A

transient error could also manifest itself as an algorithmic
or a temporary error. If the transient error is not
detected (e.g. an erroneous state occurs but is undetected
by parity checks and no illegal instruction signal is
generated) then the erroneous state would hopefully be
detected as an algorithmic failure when the result of the
computation is tested for acceptance at the end of the
recovery block.

A hardware cache (or software equivalent (Horning
1974, Randell 1975)) may be used to assist in state saving;
see 8.3.2 above.

Tasks will interact in various ways and the
correct restoration of system state is made more complicated
when state changes in one task are propagated to another.
Suppose task A generates and transmits data to task B at
some time t. If an error is subsequently detected in task
A, it might be necessary to restore task A to a state that
existed before time t. However, it cannot be guaranteed
that the data in task B is correct, and so task B must also
be restored to a state that existed before time t.
Restoration of state has to be propagated from task A to
task B. Further propagation of state restoration may be
necessary if task B has communicated with other tasks since
the last checkpoint. If the checkpoints stored are poorly
coordinated, it is possible for a disastrous avalanche of
uncontrollable activity to propagate through the system -
the Domino Effect.

There are several approaches to avoiding the
Domino Effect. One approach is to abandon the strictly
backward error recovery technique implied by the use of
checkpointing, and to compensate for the failure. This
approach is only applicable when interactions need not be
undone, and is not a mechanism that can be generally
applied.

A second approach attempts to coordinate the
backward recovery actions of interacting processes by
encapsulating process interactions in a conversation
(Randell 1975). All processes engaged in a conversation

must satisfy their respective acceptance tests before any of
the processes are allowed to exit the conversation. Should
the acceptance test of any process fail, all processes in
the conversation are returned to the point where they
entered the conversation to resume execution. This
"synchronisation of conversation exit", together with the
requirement that conversations be nested, is sufficient to
prevent the Domino Effect occurring. This approach has a
number of disadvantages. Firstly, the linking of recovery
blocks of separately designed processes can result in
deadlock. Designing the conversation and corresponding
processes as one module of a program overcomes the problem
of deadlock, but the independent design of individual
processes is compromised. Secondly, the requirement for the
synchronisation of processes at the exit of a conversation
is likely to lead to unacceptably inefficient run-time
performance, even in the absence of errors.

In all but the simplest systems, the volume of
data required to be saved for a complete checkpoint, and the
time taken to save and restore the data, would be
prohibitively large. It is far better to save only changes
to system critical data so that state restoration involves
only the changes that have been made to this critical data.
A software feature (see Horning 1974 and Randell 1975) and a
hardware device (see Anderson 1976 and Lee 1980) have been
proposed to implement this incremental saving of system
state changes and the automatic restoration of system state
when necessary. The software feature is termed a <u>recovery</u>
<u>block</u> and provides facilities for the detection of failures
(an acceptance test which must be passed successfully) and
reconfiguration (a set of alternate algorithms which are
substituted for the primary algorithm should an internal
error occur). The hardware device is a recovery cache which
holds the data describing the state of the system upon entry
to a recovery block, thus saving the old values of variables
that are subsequently modified. If the acceptance test
fails and restoration to the prior state is required, it is
relatively easy to recover the old values of modified

variables from the recovery cache, and return the system to
the state that existed upon entry to the recovery block. An
alternative algorithm is then tried or a simple retry may be
performed depending on the type of error that occurred.

8.4.3 Error detection

Errors and faults can arise in very many different
situations. It is not intended to describe exhaustively all
possible erroneous situations and how they may be detected,
but to give a broad overview of the detection methods that
may be used for both hardware faults and software errors and
to explain how Ada helps with error detection.

In general errors and faults can only be detected
by using redundancy. Hardware methods for detecting faults
involve only the use of spatial redundancy. That is, the
system includes hardware which detects errors but does not
contribute to the functionality of the system, such as
parity encoders and checkers, replications of the basic
hardware, and voting and synchronisation mechanisms in
triple modular redundancy (TMR) systems. With the ever
decreasing cost of hardware, TMR and similar methods are
viable for systems that require high levels of resilience.
They provide the ability to detect almost all faults, the
only exceptions being when the voting hardware fails as this
is not normally triplicated.

Methods involving replication of hardware but not
software do not cope with design or manufacturing errors in
either hardware or software because all the replicated
hardware will produce the same, perhaps incorrect, result.
These errors will have to be detected by software and in
this overview can be grouped together in the same class of
errors. The methods for detecting these errors involve both
spatial and time redundancy. Time redundancy is exhibited
by the system performing computations that do not contribute
to its functionality, e.g. time-out initiation and
cancellation and execution of reasonableness checks on
outputs. An example of the spatial redundancy in systems
using software error detection is the space allocated to

that error detection software.

Ada does provide a certain amount of error
detection software. The most notable facility is the
exception which allows the programmer to write code for
handling errors that have been anticipated or are thought to
be possible. These include memory overflow, constraint
errors and errors in handling input and output. In order for
these checks to be carried out, the Ada compiler adds code
to the program for the necessary checks. This can be a
considerable overhead in execution time when the program is
running correctly and it might be wise to restrict the
number of checks to those places where an error can, or is
likely to, happen. A high quality Ada compiler might be able
to carry out some of the necessary optimisations.

Another class of error detection is the explicit
programming of checking packages or routines, designed to be
called at critical points in the execution of the system.
This is of course a much higher level of checking than those
described above but can be very useful to check consistency
of inputs and outputs. In Ada, the conditional entry call,
and delay alternatives to select statements, can be used to
ensure that a task does not wait for ever for a rendezvous
that is never likely to succeed.

The subject of error detection is far too large to
study in detail in this section, but it is hoped that the
reader will appreciate that error and fault detection can be
both comprehensive and reasonably efficient in both space
and time although, like all matters relating to reliable
systems, the initial cost of developing the necessary
hardware and software can be high.

8.5 ADA SPECIFIC APPROACHES

It is possible to cope with many recovery and
reconfiguration situations from within an Ada program. This
section proposes methods which can be used to implement
recovery of data, recovery from errors, and operator
controlled reconfiguration and upgrading. These methods are
intended to be used in conjunction with some of the hardware

related approaches described above. They do allow the
software designer more freedom in designing error recovery
procedures specific to his application without too much
recourse to hardware. The recovery unit is assumed to be a
task or a group of tasks.

8.5.1 Data Saving and Recovery

When recovering from a failure it is necessary to
be able to restart the task without losing its crucial data.
The local data of a task can be sufficient to enable
recovery to a similar, if not identical, state to that
before the task failed. However, in a multi-processor system
a failure may mean that the failed task's memory is no
longer accessible. It is necessary to save state on a
different hardware node, which is a different virtual node,
so that state can be recovered after a hardware node
failure. We briefly mention some of the problems involved in
doing this and describe how rendezvous can be used to save
and restore state and data in both static and dynamic
configurations.

8.5.2 Ways in which data can be lost

There are many ways of losing data in a multiprocessor system and we should be concerned with all of
them. However, listed here are those that are considered to
be the most important:

a) Lost rendezvous data

Data can be lost due to errors in the underlying
communications subsystem. This could be prevented by the
run-time system, otherwise a good way of programming for
this eventuality is to have timeouts on entry calls and
retry the rendezvous if a rendezvous does not take place.
This does not cope with the problem of losing data while
passing parameters between tasks, which can only be
prevented by the run-time system or a lower level mechanism.

If the calling task fails during a rendezvous, any
data lost cannot be recovered as the called task will

continue unaffected, but the rendezvous may be retried after
recovery. The called task should be rolled back accordingly.

If the called task fails during rendezvous, the
calling task will have TASKING_ERROR raised and so recovery
can be programmed into the system.

b) Lost single task

If a single task is lost due to one processor in a
hardware node (cluster) going down (or some other reason)
then recovery may be possible in the same cluster as all
data from the task will still be accessible. Recovery within
the cluster is recommended as some of the other tasks may
share data with the failed task. Note that register state
and other hardware information will be lost which may make
recovery more difficult.

c) Lost hardware node

If an entire hardware node is lost then every task
that was executing on that node will have to be restarted.
For each task to be restarted, it is necessary to recover
the data of that task from some other hardware node.

d) Lost nested task of a task

If the child of a task is lost then it is
necessary to restart that child within the scope of the
parent. This should be no problem as long as the recovery is
programmed into the parent task.

e) Lost I/O data

Some systems get regular input values from
external sources and do not necessarily mind if some of
these inputs are lost because they can work on the most
recent input. Other systems may need to act on every input.
If input values are lost because a task has gone down and a
replacement is not yet active, then the only way of ensuring
that no inputs are lost is to rely on the run-time system to
buffer input until it is accepted by the Ada program.

Once output data has been sent by the Ada program, it is up to the run-time system to ensure that it reaches its destination.

8.5.3 Saving and restoring state
in a static configuration

If there is no dynamic recovery available in the system it will not be possible to have standby tasks and so it is necessary to save state by storing important information about the system and reading this information when the system is restarted from scratch. Because the memory in which this information is stored may go down, a duplicate copy of the state information will have to be stored in a different part of the system. Section 8.5.4 describes a method for doing this.

This method will involve a considerable amount of programming but will be fairly resilient unless there has been a serious crash involving all the processors on which the state information is stored. The state information could be used to pass control to different parts of the system in order that the system could restart execution from a state similar to that in which it crashed.

8.5.4 Dynamic state saving and recovery

State saving can be carried out in a dynamically reconfigurable system by having standby tasks communicating with the active task at various stages of operation so that important information can be kept up to date in the inactive (standby) task. A simple method of doing this would be to use a similar recovery procedure to that used in the static case by recreating any active task after it has failed and by reading the state information back from the passive task before continuing execution. Recovery would take a long time in anything but a very small system and so here we propose that the standby task can become the active task after a failure and a new standby can be created. Switchover will be much faster and equally resilient.

Each task has a number of entry points so that
data transfer can be accomplished by rendezvous used solely
for this purpose and the tasks can be programmed in such a
way that once the standby task becomes active a new standby
is created in order to pass state information to a known
task. There will have to be a controlling task (or the run-
time system) which switches a task from the standby to
active mode. By referring to tasks via access types, the
name of the standby and the active task can be swapped after
a recovery so that other tasks can rendezvous with the new
active task.

For some tasks that are purely passive, such as a
buffer task between a producer and a consumer, it is not
necessary to keep a standby task in exactly the same state
as the active task as we are interested only in the data
contained in the task. If we considered a buffer task then
the easiest way of maintaining a secure buffer would be to
keep a copy of the data and the state of the producer and
consumer tasks. When the producer sends a data item to the
buffer it also sends the item to the backup buffer and when
the consumer has actually used the current item, it informs
the backup that the next item can be removed from the
buffer. If the buffer task fails, its reinitialisation will
include a rendezvous with the backup buffer task to copy the
current state of the buffer and the necessary data. If the
backup task fails then, when it is recreated, it can
reinitialise its data from the main buffer task.

This method will cope with failures in the
consumer task as the backup task is not updated until the
current item has been consumed, but it is not possible to
guarantee against loss of one data item if the producer task
fails. A system could be devised for some applications that
would allow the input data to the producer to be wound back.
This is possible by keeping a count on the data received by
the buffer or the consumer.

8.5.5 Recovery from faults

Programmed recovery from failures on a multiprocessor system takes place through task replacement. Replacement is intended to mean the failed task will not be restarted but another task will run in its place. This new task may either be newly created or be an existing task made active and it may or may not have an identical algorithm to the failed task.

Swapping between tasks has already been mentioned above, but in general this will not be resilient enough. The standby task may fail and so a mechanism must be available for recreating this task without affecting the active task. Because Ada states that an attempted rendezvous with a failed (terminated) task will cause TASKING_ERROR to be raised in the calling task, a mechanism will have to be provided in the run-time system to hold up the active task while a new standby task is being created. There is a problem with the naming of tasks after recreation. The new active task will have been called something like STANDBY, which will cause problems for external rendezvous. We could get round this problem by using task access types and reassigning the values of STANDBY and ACTIVE after a failure. We would then have the following definitions:

```
task type ACTIVE_OR_STANDBY is
    -- Entry declarations
end ACTIVE_OR_STANDBY;
type ACCESS_A_OR_S is access ACTIVE_OR_STANDBY;
ACTIVE, STANDBY : ACCESS_A_OR_S;
```

The tasks would be created by the assignments:

```
STANDBY := new ACTIVE_OR_STANDBY;
ACTIVE  := new ACTIVE_OR_STANDBY;
```

and after a failure of an active task we would carry out the following operations:

```
        ACTIVE := STANDBY;
          -- new ACTIVE is the old STANDBY
        STANDBY := new ACTIVE_OR_STANDBY;
          -- create a new STANDBY
        ACTIVE.STANDBY_TO_ACTIVE;
          -- call appropriate entry to activate ACTIVE
```

This means that the tasks themselves will not call a
rendezvous to create a new active task.

The method described so far is one where two
tasks, or possibly more if the complexity can be tolerated
for added resilience, are continuously running and
communicating with one another. In a large system the amount
of data that would have to be passed between the tasks,
which will not be sharing memory, may be prohibitively
large. Therefore we need a method of task replacement
independent of state saving. The method should be capable of
being used for replacement of a task by an identical one,
for graceful degradation where full functionality is not
required after a serious hardware failure, and for algorithm
replacement after a software error.

The requirements cited above are ambitious and if
they were all to be incorporated into a single method,
potentially simple programs would become extremely complex.
It is intended briefly to discuss methods for handling the
different cases and to propose solutions which are specific
to particular problem classes but which could be generalised
if necessary.

8.5.5.1 Replacement of tasks with identical ones

This method is the simplest and is useful in many
cases where tasks have to be restarted after a hardware
failure but the state of the task either does not matter or
can be recovered from another part of the program.

It is essential that tasks can communicate with
one another at all times when a system is running, but if a
task fails there will be a temporary loss of communication
which must be rectified by the system. The method outlined

here allows the recovery of the communications links to be
described at the Ada source level by recreating the failed
task and by informing all those tasks that make entry calls
to the failed task of its new identity. This idea can be
implemented using task access types and special rendezvous.

Every task type in the program has an access type
to allow other tasks to refer to a task by a variable name:

```
          task type ONE is
               -- entry declarations
          end ONE;
          type ACCESS_ONE is access ONE;
```

```
          ONE_NAME: ACCESS_ONE;
```

Now a task can be recreated by making the
assignment ONE_NAME := new ONE; This will of course make it
impossible to access the old task ONE and so any pending
rendezvous with the old task will never take place.

There are two important features to consider when
implementing the method, namely the semantics of Ada's
rendezvous and the method of recovery.

The rendezvous is well defined in the Ada
reference manual and particular consideration should be
given to the conditions under which exceptions are raised.
We use these rules to build up the exception handlers and
rendezvous needed to cope with task failures. All tasks that
call an entry will need an exception handler for
TASKING_ERROR in which any necessary recovery statements are
included. In tasks that are accepting entries, no exception
is raised when the calling task fails and so it is necessary
to include a select statement containing any rendezvous for
recovery that is required. It is essential to take great
care to avoid deadlocks after recovery and to guarantee the
correct order of execution of rendezvous.

8.5.5.2 Applicability of this method to the virtual node approach

This section gives a very brief overview of the problems involved in using the method described above with the virtual node approach.

One of the primary assumptions made in the virtual node approach is that construction of the system is an entirely off-line process. This implies that there is no run-time reconfiguration or reallocation of code and data. It is also assumed that neither code nor data may be directly accessed by any task outside the virtual node in which that code or data has been declared. In the case of code it will be necessary to repeat code that is used by more than one virtual node (e.g. library packages) and data sharing between virtual nodes must take place via server tasks. We allow shared data but it will require much less work if there is none. The code for each task will have to be resident on more than one processor as if it was shared between virtual nodes, but only active on one. This will allow restarting of tasks up to a certain limit without moving any code, but it will still be necessary to re-route the communications between tasks.

In an Ada program which uses access types (e.g. the fault tolerant system described above), it is assumed that there is only one heap. Clearly, the heap must be partitioned between processors; tasks should have access to that part of the heap local to their particular virtual node. The virtual node approach restricts the use of access types across virtual node boundaries to access tasks; no other access types may be passed to remote virtual nodes. This is quite sufficient for the needs of dynamic reconfiguration.

8.5.6 Graceful degradation

If there are not enough hardware resources available to run the entire program after a serious hardware failure then it may be necessary to reconfigure the program in such a way that some facilities are no longer available

but the program will still run safely. This is an
application dependent problem as the specific requirements
for degradation cannot be generalised; however there are a
number of points worth considering when designing a system
for degradation.

After a failure from which total recovery cannot
be achieved, the run-time system or a recovery task will
have to start a task designed to carry out the degradation
of the system. It will also have to cope with controlling
communication during the degradation phase as parts of the
system may become inaccessible for a short time. The task
carrying out the degradation may have to stop some tasks and
replace them with other simpler ones and may also have to
restart tasks that were stopped by the hardware failure.
This will be a complex process and will involve a
considerable number of entries in many of the tasks to
enable the system to be restarted in a consistent state. The
method described above could be used for the task
replacement and for controlling communication during the
degradation phase.

8.5.7 Algorithm replacement

The obvious way to carry out algorithm replacement
is to have more than one task body for a particular task
specification. However, this is not allowed by Ada and, if
such an extension were to be made, the program construction
system and the run-time system would become extremely
complex. Two alternative and undoubtedly more practical
solutions are:

a) have two tasks whose specifications are the same
   but which have different names and different
   algorithms within the body, or

b) have a task with two or more "real" bodies
   incorporated within the task body with a
   rendezvous to allow body selection when the task
   is started, hence allowing the use of the standard
   method of task replacement.

The first solution seems the cleaner although it will only work for active tasks where no accept statements are executed since the task will have changed its name and so entry calls to it would be impossible. There are two ways of getting round this problem:

i) The calling task must be aware of the replacement and be coded accordingly:

```
        if REPLACED then REPLACEMENT.ENTRY(...);
                 else ORIGINAL.ENTRY(...);
        end if;
```

There could be a rendezvous in the calling task that is called when the task has been replaced or been switched back to the original to toggle the value of REPLACED. It is possible to switch back to the original by creating a new version using the basic access type method or just trying again.

ii) Only replace active tasks.

Passive tasks can be recoded as active tasks by introducing an interface task, and so this restriction does not limit the power of the method. Note that the interface task can be protected by using the state saving method or by identical task replacement.

8.5.8 State restoration

After the failure of a task whose state has been saved at particular checkpoints, it is necessary to go back to the correct part of the program to continue with the data from the previous checkpoint. This can be programmed either by using loops and conditional statements as long as no potentially incorrect data has been passed out of the task via rendezvous. If this is the case then it may be necessary to wind back other tasks to a consistent state. This could be achieved by having special rendezvous to pass messages informing tasks that they must wind back to a specific point or by using one of the hardware related methods discussed earlier. This adds another level of complexity and so should be kept to a minimum. Where possible, checkpoints and acceptance tests should be put immediately before all points in any task where information is passed out of the task.

8.6 DYNAMIC UPGRADING AND RECONFIGURATION

This section is concerned with the dynamic reconfiguration of Ada programs for the purpose of upgrading or enhancement. This function is desirable for many real-time systems, and is in fact essential for certain critical systems, parts of which are stable and must not be stopped, whilst other parts are subject to amendment; an example of this is the electric power telecontrol system described in Chapter 2.

Reconfiguration of this kind is expected at infrequent intervals, and the point at which it is performed is decided by the human operator, at a convenient time - not as a means of recovery in response to some failure. The new units to be introduced will therefore be fully tested and loaded in advance, allowing the reconfiguration operation itself to be relatively short.

Reconfiguration can sometimes be performed by the addition of complete virtual nodes and the subsequent amendment of external references to the affected units. However, in some systems, processing must not be interrupted during the reconfiguration.

8.6.1 Objective

The aim of dynamic upgrading is the amendment of a running Ada program by the addition or deletion of program units. In particular, any new units should not be restricted to existing unit types: in this respect, complete flexibility is required. The amendment process should ideally be performed without:

- stopping the execution of unaffected parts of the program;
- damaging the behaviour of the affected parts;
- causing recompilation of unaffected existing units;

- compromising type checking;
- introducing unacceptable overheads or
  inefficiencies.

It is expected that a system is constructed as a
collection of independent virtual nodes, each having both
visible and invisible (nested) entries. It is desirable
that the full power of dynamic tasking is not used (e.g. the
passing of a node's private task as a parameter to a remote
node's entry) since such use widens the inter-node interface
and is likely to produce unpredictable results when entire
nodes are deleted or substituted.

8.6.2 Assumptions

It is assumed that the construction system
includes a configuration manager module which, in
cooperation with the human operator, maintains a description
of the application system configuration, and amends it to
effect changes. The application system itself should have
read-only access to this description in order to adjust
itself to correspond to it.

The virtual node is chosen as the unit of
reconfiguration because of its well-defined and controllable
interface, and its representation as an Ada program unit
allows the exploitation of useful features of the language.

It is therefore expected that the virtual node
will be represented by a group of Ada tasks, with the
outermost level also being a task, since this has many
qualities essential to the proposed method:

1) It can be subject to access types.
2) It can be dynamically created and destroyed, as a
   true program object.
3) It has a limited interface, containing only
   procedure-like entries. (This defines the form of
   the facilities it provides to its callers, though
   not that of the calls which it can initiate
   itself.)

4) Task identities can be passed as parameters.

5) Tasks are an automatically imposed limit to the propagation of exceptions.

6) It has a body which can contain nested tasks and statements. It is intended that the nested tasks perform the application function (in any required internal arrangement) whilst the outermost task is essentially for configuration purposes and for the transfer of data to other parts of the system.

The other logical candidate for virtual node representation is the package but much of its flexibility is apparent only during compilation; although it constitutes a compilation unit in its own right, and can be made generic, it is not a true program object, and cannot be manipulated as such. In particular, it cannot be dynamically created or destroyed. However, using a task for virtual node representation can be made easier by embedding a task in a package, effectively allowing it to be used as a compilation unit, and allowing the use of generics.

The flexibility of the package interface is largely unused. Nodes are not permitted to share data, so the contents of the visible part of a package must be severely limited: only type definitions, tasks, and subprograms may appear there.

Since calls to a node must be directed to its outermost entries, and these are under the exclusive control of the node task itself, there is a danger of a bottleneck forming if the node is large, or calls are very frequent. This can generally be overcome by system design and care in the allocation of processing resources to such nodes.

The method described here also makes assumptions about the run-time system's representation of tasks and their entries; these will be covered below.

8.6.3 Visibility

Ada's naming and visibility rules, whilst very
effective in ensuring consistency throughout a collection of
separately compiled units, are over-restrictive for the
purposes of reconfiguration.

In order for one unit to use another in any way,
it must know its name, which implies that the called unit's
specification must be declared first, possibly in a previous
compilation. Where called units are named via access types,
then at least this access type must be declared before the
caller.

If an entirely new unit is to be introduced to a
program without recompilation of all existing units which
are to call it, then some indirect naming scheme is
required, making the units completely independent of each
other.

This can be provided by the use of access types:
one specifically for each task type, and a general one to
which all others can be translated by instances of the predefined generic function UNCHECKED_CONVERSION.

Both the specific and general access types must be
made available to the tasks; for correct compilation, task
identities of the specific kind must appear in entry calls,
whereas any identity passed to the configuration manager
must be of the general access type. Since all identities
are access values to task types, there need be no confusion
regarding their interpretation.

This necessarily reduces type checking, but in
practice we are concerned with the consistency of parameter
types in entry calls; this will be preserved by the method.
The run-time system need not necessarily hold data type
information, since in practice, the correspondence of
parameter types in the replaced and the replacement tasks
will be checked at an early stage in the development of the
replacement. It is envisaged that this checking would be
purely automatic - the operator must clearly be given no
opportunity to avoid it.

8.6.4 Reconfiguration

Initially, each task holds valid access values for each of its correspondents. Removal involves the setting of a task as 'terminated'; calls to it from this point on will cause TASKING_ERROR to be raised in the caller. In handling TASKING_ERROR, the caller calls the configuration manager, giving the identity of the called task, and is given in return the identity of its replacement, which is already installed and running, but as yet unknown to the rest of the system. The caller then repeats its original call, this time to the new task.

As stated above, type conversions are employed to enable the configuration manager to deal with many task types through one common entry. The calling sequence will be similar to the following, where GENERAL and SPECIFIC are instantiations of the generic function UNCHECKED_CONVERSION and IDENT and REMOTE_NODE are node identities of the general and specific types respectively:

```
loop
  begin
    REMOTE_NODE.ENTRY_NAME(...);
    -- Statements to follow successful call.
    exit;
  exception
    when TASKING_ERROR =>
      IDENT := GENERAL(REMOTE_NODE);
      CONFIGURATION_MANAGER.NEW_ID(IDENT);
      REMOTE_NODE := SPECIFIC(IDENT);
  end;
end loop;
```

Deletion of tasks can be achieved either by the introduction of a 'null task', which simply accepts its entries and returns some default value, or else by returning NULL as the new task identity. In the first case, the null task may later be replaced.

Until all references to the replaced task have been amended in this way, the configuration manager must continue to hold its identity, in order to perform the

mapping. If only one copy of any identity is permitted per
virtual node, held as a variable global to any nested tasks,
then all references will be amended after any one nested
task has called for the new identity. However, this raises
the problem of concurrent access of the identities; it is
preferable to insist that each variable is private, and used
by only one task. In this case the configuration manager
must hold the old identity indefinitely, though this is
unlikely to be more than a small overhead.

The configuration manager is clearly the most
complex part of the scheme; in some respects it behaves like
a program unit as it can be called by the nodes themselves.
There must be feedback to the development of the replacement
nodes and their checking, but here we are only concerned
with the problems of the upgrading process.

The part of the configuration manager for dynamic
upgrading must supply information to the running program
units and should be kept small, since it will form part of
the run-time support system. Its specification will be that
of a task, the various facilities it will support being
entries to ensure mutual exclusion for the updating of the
system description data structures.

8.6.5 Damage to Unaffected Program Units

It is necessary to handle the removal of a task to
which entry calls are pending. The mechanism that terminates
the task must ensure that correct Ada semantics are
maintained - pending calls should result in TASKING_ERROR,
so this case can be treated in the same way as a call which
is made after termination.

Due to the nature of distributed systems, it is
likely that calls between virtual nodes will be either
conditional or timed, depending on context. In addition, it
is necessary for calls to be enveloped in an exception
handler. This traps exceptions raised by calling those
units that are in some disrupted state, so that they are not
propagated throughout the caller.

8.6.6 State Transfer

There are cases in which some state information held by the worker task must be transferred to the standby in order to maintain the function of the system. An example is the enhancement of a unit which maintains a database.

The scope rules of the language do not allow external access directly to the nested, local variables of a unit, and in any case it is convenient to reclaim all resources allocated to the replaced unit.

A straightforward solution is to hold the critical data externally to the node by placing it in a library package. Since the contents of this package are logically private to their node, only that node should have access via a "with" clause. If this is the case, then there can be no conflict due to concurrent access (except between tasks in that one node). A replacement node (with the appropriate "with" clause) must not use the data until the replaced node is terminated.

This scheme is sufficient for updating in situ; however recovery after certain failures may involve more than one physical node. In such cases, the library package data must be transferred to the local memory of the replacement node. If this cannot be done, then complete recovery is not possible, and backup or default values must be used. Under no circumstances should memory accesses be attempted.

There is no overhead in the use of the package; it is simply a naming strategy, and in most cases would not even have a body. Where the data has a complex structure, it would be convenient to include access procedures in the package to raise the level of abstraction of operations in the node. These procedures might include acceptance tests to check the function of the task.

8.6.7 Parameter Data Type Checking

Ensuring consistency between the replaced and the replacement tasks is in fact relatively simple, subject to one restriction:

- The specification of the replacement task must contain entry declarations identical to all of those in the replaced task.

In addition, it may contain further entry declarations, which will be inaccessible to previously compiled units. Where several new units are introduced together, their compilation order will allow them to communicate via these new entries.

If a further (reasonable) rule is imposed, that the entries common to both tasks appear in the same order, and before the additional declarations, then implementation will require little or no complication. The most likely schemes used to implement entries will be dependent on offsets within some task context variable; these will probably be unaffected by additional entry declarations after the common ones, and the ordering will ensure the correspondence of the replacement entries with the originals.

8.6.8 Termination of Tasks

The mechanism used to warn a calling task of the termination of a replaced task need not introduce any great overhead. A check value might be held with the task instance and with any access value to it. Upon each access to the task, the values are compared, and must correspond for a valid identity.

To register a task as terminated involves only the resetting of the check value in the instance itself - all attempted calls from then on will not use valid identities. A function of the run-time system would be to interpret this failure as termination and raise TASKING_ERROR in the caller.

This method avoids the unpredictable overhead of locating and amending all references to a task from all

units in the system. It is also independent of the address
part of the value; in the case of a distributed system this
may well include a machine identity. The major overhead is
in the size of the access value, since it is now more than
just an address, and may have doubled in size. However, the
scheme can be applied equally effectively to all access
types, indicating the presence or removal of the referenced
object from the system. This is desirable from the point of
view of consistency of representation for all access types.

8.6.9 Further Development

The scheme described above will allow the
replacement of tasks in a running Ada program. For
simplicity, it is intended for use only at the level of
virtual nodes, i.e. the top level of a system, although the
same actions could be applied for any group of tasks.
However care should be taken with tasks that share global
data, since the forced termination of tasks may produce
inconsistencies or deadlocks.

The grain of reconfiguration is limited to tasks,
rather than entries. This is not fully flexible, since
every reference to a task must be redirected to its
replacement - there can be no selective replacement of a
task allowing some parts of the program to continue to use
the original, as in Conic (Magee & Kramer, 1983). This
limitation is offset by the simplicity of the method: its
use is relatively transparent, and it should be
implementable efficiently in an existing Ada system.

Further flexibility would require some indirect
naming scheme at the entry level - a facility not available
in Ada, and therefore one that could not be reflected simply
in a program. Such a scheme would probably have to be
supported entirely by the run-time system.

8.7 <u>CONCLUSIONS</u>

Many of the issues discussed in this chapter are current research topics and generalised approaches have not yet been developed. It would therefore be unreasonable to expect Ada to embody such approaches. However, where approaches have been suggested in this chapter, Ada has been found to be an appropriate notation in which to code the approaches. This sometimes requires the use of unchecked conversion and/or packages interfacing to the run-time system. It must be accepted that any effect of hardware failure or transients on the running of an Ada program in some sense violates the semantics of Ada. Even to abort a task on a faulty node goes beyond the language definition. In minor ways multiprocessor systems are themselves bound to violate the strictest interpretation of the language definition, in that, for example, it is impossible to guarantee the instantaneous termination of all the dependent tasks of a task at the moment it is aborted.

In most approaches in this chapter, spectra exist between implementations in which most of the approach is represented in the application software and implementations in which most of the approach is embedded in the run-time system and/or the hardware. The former is likely to involve greater development costs and run-time overhead than the latter, but should provide greater flexibility. In most cases the virtual node (not originally intended for dynamically reconfigurable systems) has been found useful as a unit of reconfiguration.

Further research in the areas of reliability and extensibility should be encouraged. There needs to be some emphasis on these areas in the European Esprit programme and national programmes, such as the UK Alvey programme. Considering that the aim of Ada is to be suitable for embedded systems requiring high reliability, it is surprising that more consideration has not been given to the possibility of fault-tolerant multiprocessor targets.

9
The MML experience

9.1 INTRODUCTION

This chapter describes the MML programming language, and its support environment (MMDS), which have been developed in Italy, by a consortium including TXT and CISE. It has largely been taken from the paper by Boari et al. (1984), which was published in IEEE Computer; we acknowledge their permission to reproduce this material.

MML attempts to provide a reasonable practical tool set for programming distributed applications with as little departure as possible from today's practice. Simplicity of use and portability are its main concerns. It is expected to cover 8-bit and 16-bit multiple-microprocessor configurations, but it is not intended to be effective for larger machines.

The main objective is to provide a programming tool for a broad range of distributed microprocessor architectures and applications. The usual program development cycle consists of application analysis, hardware prototype design or selection, software development and testing on a host computer (the Micro Development System, or MDS), and program and prototype integration for overall real-time testing.

Hardware is frequently chosen before software design, so the designer can fully specify allocation of program modules to memory at compilation, linking, or loading time. However, software can be developed for a partial prototype, since an MDS can lend its resources, such as memory and CPU, to the prototype for emulation.

Similarly, our development system for multi-microprocessors (called the Multi-Micro Programming Line, MML) is based on the host-target approach, but the target can be any multi-micro configuration out of an open set of supported architectures. As a first requirement, MML can be retargeted to prototype systems of any reasonable architecture. Reorienting MML to a different architecture requires a fraction of the initial development cost. Within one architecture, configuration may differ considerably, ranging from a single processor to various forms of tightly or loosely coupled multiple microprocessors. Different processors may be present in the same configuration.

To take full advantage of multi-micro systems, the designer should not freeze the prototype configuration ahead of software design. He should be free to experiment with various configurations without having to rewrite his software or, even worse, to redesign the runtime support. Moreover, the allocation of hardware resources to functions should be the designer's responsibility. Thus, a second requirement for MML is that prototype configuration and allocation are design variables that should be exploited to meet such requirements as real-time response or system availability and to optimise the cost-effectiveness of resources.

The first two requirements clearly separate program description (data and algorithms) from hardware description (configuration). As a third requirement, MML provides specific tools for hardware description and resource allocation. MML includes a language and a compiler for process and procedure description, plus facilities for hardware configuration description, resource allocation, run-time system configuration, debugging, and execution control. MML allows software development without reliance on the final prototype. If the prototype does not exist, the host computer could be assigned to run all processes for software testing.

Since microprocessors are generally used to control I/O equipment (sensors, actuators, and peripherals),

effective tools for I/O programming and real-time response
must be provided. Two paths toward a solution are possible:

- Assign I/O operations to assembly-language encoded
  modules that interface with higher level modules,
  as normally done with such sequential system
  languages for microprocessors as PL/M (Intel
  1977a) and PLZ-SYS (Conway et al. 1979).
- Express I/O operations in high-level language.
  However, the high-level stream-oriented I/O, such
  as in Pascal, is not adequate for embedded
  microprocessor applications.

The variety of peripheral chips and the need to be
retargetable complicate the problem. Assigning I/O
operations to modules coded in assembly language has the
unpleasant effect of reducing machine independence, since
the assembly languages of micros differ considerably. The
economy of suppressing assembly-language programming made us
opt to express I/O operations in high-level language.
Consequently, MML's language offers elementary facilities
for programming all sorts of I/O devices at a low level by
allowing the addressing of peripherals and the control of
interrupts.

To ensure real-time response to time-critical
events, four techniques enacted at four levels can be
joined:

- Hardware level: either increasing the actual
  parallelism of the target system by adding
  microprocessors to the net until eventually each
  process is executed on a dedicated processor or
  providing fast interprocessor communications where
  required. Broadband channels are achieved by
  tightly connecting micros via shared memories, a
  solution offered by most architectures, since
  configuration changes do not impact the source
  program.

- Allocation level: at system configuration time,
  assigning fixed pathways to intercommunicating
  processes having stringent time requirements.
  Other noncritical processes must contend for
  channels.
- Program level: ensuring top-priority to I/O
  interrupts on multitasked micros by introducing
  interrupt procedures automatically invoked when
  certain interrupt signals occur.
- Translation level: increasing the actual execution
  speed of object code. Processes can be translated
  to the faster machine code or interpreted.

9.2 THE MULTI-MICRO PROGRAMMING LINE

MML is a portable software tool set for developing
concurrent distributed programs for multiple
microprocessors. As shown in Figure 9.1, it consists of a
program development tool set called the Multi-Micro
Development System (MMDS), written in Pascal and currently
hosted by a PDP-11/34, and a run-time system (RTS).

MML includes a language and a compiler for process
and procedure definition, plus facilities for hardware
configuration description, resource allocation, run-time
system construction, debugging, and execution control.

The language: sequential and concurrent features.

An MML program consists of a fixed number of
processes called sequences, which start simultaneously,
exist forever, and cooperate to accomplish certain specific
tasks.

The communication and synchronisation mechanisms
of MML were determined by the following two requirements:
- The design of the application software must be as
  independent as possible from the multiple-
  microprocessor architecture. The mapping of
  processes to processors, of data and algorithms to
  memories, and of logical to physical

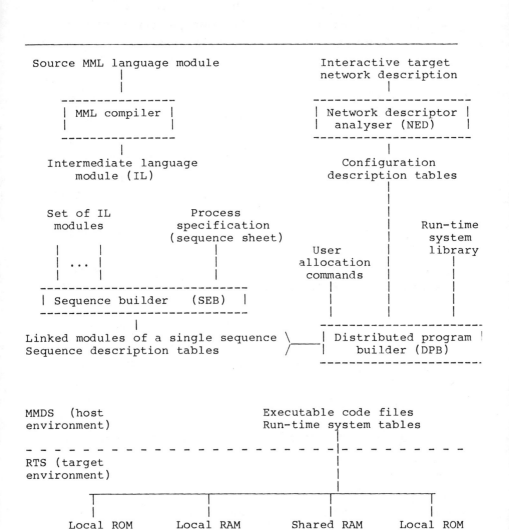

Source MML language module   Interactive target
            | network description
            | |
    ------------------   ------------------------
    | MML compiler | | Network descriptor |
    | | | analyser (NED) |
    ------------------   ------------------------
            | |
    Intermediate language   Configuration
        module (IL)   description tables
                                               |
                                               |
    Set of IL   Process |
    modules   specification | Run-time
                   (sequence sheet) | system
     | | | User | library
     | ...| | allocation |
     | | | commands | |
    ------------------------------ | |
    | Sequence builder   (SEB) | | |
    ------------------------------ | |
            | ------------------------
Linked modules of a single sequence ___| Distributed program |
Sequence description tables   / | builder (DPB) |

MMDS (host   Executable code files
environment)   Run-time system tables
                                        |
- - - - - - - - - - - - - - - - - - - -|- - - - - - - -
RTS (target |
environment) |
                                        |
        _____|_____
        | | | |
    Local ROM   Local RAM   Shared RAM   Local ROM
    memory   memory   memory   memory
        | | | |
    ===================== | ========
    local bus | | | local
                   | | | bus
            processor | processor
                   | | |
        ===
                        global bus

              Figure 9.1 MML System Overview

interprocessor channels is defined in the
allocation phase following the design of
application software. Therefore, the communication
and synchronisation must be efficiently
implemented on a variety of architectures, ranging
from multiple-microprocessor structures with
shared memory to truly distributed systems.
- To simplify concurrent programming, one should
choose either the global memory or the message-
passing model of communication, but not both. We
chose the latter in the "remote procedure call"
form.

New proposals available at the time that seemed to
satisfy the second requirement included communicating
sequential processes (Hoare 1978), distributed processes
(Brinch Hansen 1978), and Ada parallel tasking (DOD 1983).
All three of them adopt a message-passing or remote
procedure call model, with the fundamental property that
synchronisation and communication are considered two
inseparable activities; that is, two processes need to be
synchronised in order to communicate. As a corollary, each
process has a local environment that cannot be accessed or
altered by any other process, a fact that enforces a rather
safe programming discipline. This so-called 'rendezvous"
concept provides a practical, unified solution to
communication and synchronisation problems. The mutual
exclusion problem, for instance, may be solved by a
rendezvous between the processes competing for resource and
the process managing the resource.

We adopted and incorporated into the MML language
the distributed processes proposal, which favours
distributed systems and qualifies as a well-balanced
combination of the established concepts of processes,
procedures, and conditional critical regions. This decision
made it possible to bring to a distributed environment much
of the consolidated methodology of global environments.
Moreover, the notion of distributed processes is rather
simple to graft onto an existing sequential language and

does not require overwhelming run-time support. This
decision, nevertheless, will be reconsidered after
additional experimentation.

In Figure 9.2, sequences "producer" and "consumer"
access a common data structure, managed in mutual exclusion
by a sequence "buffer". Each sequence is made of one or more
separately compilable modules, as described in a sequence
sheet.

The sequence sheet also lists:
- the controlled procedures it supplies (these
  procedures can be invoked by other sequences);
- the controlled procedures belonging to other
  sequences that the sequence calls;
- optionally, the initial procedure that begins
  execution of the sequence at system start-up. If
  the indication is missing, the sequence remains
  idle until one of its controlled procedures is
  invoked by another sequence.

```
P1 sequence                        BUFFER sequence
   owns producer_module               owns buffer_module
   calls BUFFER.put                   supplies put, get
   starts producer_init               starts buffer_init
end P1                             end BUFFER

C1 sequence                        C2 sequence
   owns consumer_code                 owns consumer_code
        consumer1_data                     consumer2_data
   calls BUFFER.get                   calls BUFFER.get
   starts consumer_init               starts consumer_init
end C1                             end C2
```

Figure 9.2   Sequence sheets defining four processes: one producer
(P1), two consumers (C1, C2), and one communication buffer (BUFFER).

The essential aspects of the modules are
illustrated in Figure 9.3. More instances of the same
sequence type can be created by replicating the Modules, as
indicated in Figure 9.4. A family of almost identical
processes can also be introduced as an array of sequences
(e.g. producer(i) denotes a sequence in a family of
producers).

Control of peripheral devices under interrupt is performed by special sequences called <u>drivers</u>. Communication between drivers and peripheral devices follows the same scheme used for communication between sequences; a peripheral device may be considered as a hardware "device sequence" whose controlled procedures, invoked by the corresponding driver, are the elementary I/O commands by which the device is operated.

I/O commands are the built-in procedures:

in (register_address:word) returns (datum:byte)
out(register_address:word,   datum:byte)

Addresses passed to <u>in</u> and <u>out</u> are absolute, but their resolution can be deferred until after the target hardware is selected during the network description and DPB phase (see Figure 9.1).

A driver sequence usually supplies controlled procedures, to be called by other sequences in order to communicate with the driver, and one or more interrupt procedures. An <u>interrupt</u> <u>procedure</u> is "called" by the device sequence through a designated interrupt signal and performs the interrupt handling operations. As an example, see the input driver illustrated in Figure 9.5.

Our choice of a sequential language, for the reasons expressed earlier, was the machine-oriented system language PLZ-SYS, a simplified and modularised Pascal. Because we did not rely heavily on any particular features of the selected language, the design philosophy of MML, if not the actual language translator, can easily accommodate a different language choice.

In view of our objectives, with the constraints of hardware available to us, PLZ-SYS was a reasonable choice. We readily recognised that PLZ could be easily extended to accommodate the requirements of interprocess communication and synchronisation. In addition, the PLZ module is a natural unit for control of storage allocation.

Program development tools and run-time support.

The MMDS integrated tool set shown in Figure 9.1 was designed with third-generation features. The MML compiler translates a source language module to an intermediate machine-independent language. The binding among intermediate language-coded modules belonging to a sequence (more generally, to a "link-unit") is performed by the sequence builder.

The allocation of sequences to processors, of modules to memory banks, and of logical interprocess channels to physical ones takes place under user direction during the distributed program building phase (DPB). Clearly, this phase required knowledge of the architecture and configuration of the target, information previously entered during the network description phase.

First, an architecture is specified, such as Tomp (Conte 1981) as shown in Figure 9.6. Then, in a conversation driven by architecture description tables, the user enters configuration details about processors, memories, interprocessor channels, and I/O devices, as shown in Figure 9.7. Finally, in the DPB phase, the user maps application programs onto target units (Figure 9.8). The output of DPB is a set of executable programs (either IL-coded or machine-coded) and some run-time tables to be used by the executive. Code can be downloaded or burned on EPROMs.

As indicated in Figure 9.8, intersequence communication is described at the logical level by channels. A channel can be handled by architecture-dependent (hardware + kernel) procedures and can be physically constituted by a shared memory bank, a serial line, or a local network. One such physical resource can be dedicated to a pair of sequences or shared by several such pairs. Mapping of logical channels to one or the other of the assumed communication facilities is decided by the application engineer or settled by default.

Another choice taking place during DPB is between code generation and interpretation of application programs.

```
producer_module module
    internal item : byte
        ...
global
    producer_init procedure
    entry ...
        BUFFER.put(item)
        ...
end
end producer_module

consumer_code module
    external item : byte   !from consumer_data!
        ...
    global
        consumer_init procedure
        entry ...
            item := BUFFER.get
            ...
        end
        ...
end consumer_code

buffer_module module
    constant N = 10
    type portion : byte
    internal IN, OUT, COUNT : integer
            B : array[N] portion
    global
        put controlled procedure (C : portion)
        entry
            if COUNT<N then B[IN] := C; IN := (IN+1) mod N
                            COUNT := COUNT+1
            else
                retest  !wait for space available in the BUFFER!
            fi
        end put
    global
        get controlled procedure returns (C : portion)
        entry
            if COUNT>0 then C := B[OUT]; OUT := (OUT+1) mod N
                            COUNT := COUNT-1
            else
                retest  !wait for item available in the BUFFER!
            fi
        end get
    global
        buffer_init procedure
        entry
            IN := OUT := COUNT := 0
        end buffer_init
end buffer_module
```

Figure 9.3. Sequence BUFFER controls the message exchange betwee
sequences by supplying procedures "put" and "get" (defined i
"buffer_module"). This sequence initiates by executing procedur

"init_buffer", which completes its action and terminates. From then on, the sequence performs put and get operations as a result of external requests. Procedures such as put and get are called controlled procedures.

The producer P1 calls the procedure put to send a message to BUFFER, and it waits until BUFFER completes execution of this procedure. Execution of put can be completed if the condition COUNT<N is satisfied; otherwise, the operation is suspended by the "retest" statement. The operation will be resumed by the BUFFER when the condition becomes true as the result of the operation get.

Sequences C1 and C2 (consumers) work similarly.

Note that BUFFER is similar to a monitor; it defines a shared data structure and the operations on it. These operations take place one at a time. After initialisation, the sequence, as a monitor, is idle between external calls.

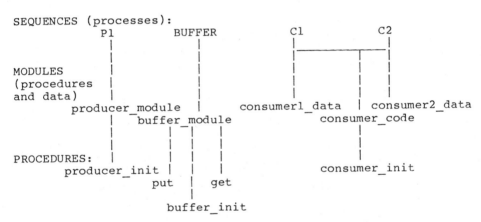

Figure 9.4   As shown in the MML scheme of Fig 9.2, the module consumer_code is replicated in two sequences. It can be shared if it is a reentrant module with no global data, and if it is allocated to a shared memory bank.

Since the same sequence occupies a different space when translated to IL or to machine-code, memory allocation is affected by the choice. To reduce the effort for producing generators for several machines, we are experimenting with the retargetable code-generation technique (Glanville & Graham 1977).

The run-time system of each target processor includes a kernel, an IL interpreter or run-time library, debugging support, and execution control support. Their functions are:

```
KEYBOARD sequence
    owns keyboard_module
    supplies read
    serves getchar      !interrupt procedure called by device!
    starts init
end KEYBOARD

keyboard_module module
    constant N = 50
    INTERRUPT-ADDR = ?   !a deferred constant to be specified
                          in the DPB phase!
    DATA_PORT_ADDR = ?   !another deferred constant: the
                          address of the device data port!
    CONTROL_PORT_ADDR = ?    !the address of the device
                              control port!
    internal BUFFER : array[N] byte
             INPTR, OUTPTR, FULL : integer
    global
        read controlled procedure returns (char : byte)
          entry
          if FULL 0 then
              CHAR := BUFFER [OUTPTR];
              OUTPTR := (OUTPTR+1) mod NFULL := FULL - 1
          else retest      !wait for CHAR available!
          fi
          end read
        getchar interrupt (INTERRUPT_ADDR) procedure
          entry
          BUFFER [INPTR] := in (DATA_PORT_ADDR)
                              !reads a byte from data port!
          INPTR := (INPTR + 1) mod N
          FULL := FULL + 1
          if FULL = n then
              retest      !wait for space available!
          fi
          end getchar
        init procedure
          entry
          INPTR := OUTPTR := FULL := 0
          startdevice
          end init
    internal
        startdevice procedure
          entry
          ! initialise the device !
        end startdevice
end KEYBOARD
```

Controlled procedure "read" is called by other sequences to communicate with the driver. If the buffer is
empty, the "read" operation is suspended on retest; otherwise, the operation is completed and a character is taken
from the buffer. In any case, "read" and "getchar" are executed in mutual exclusion. Priority is given to the execution of interrupt procedure "getchar" over "read" procedure
to handle interrupts as soon as possible.

Figure 9.5

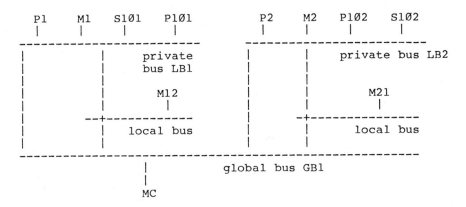

Figure 9.6   A two processor prototype of Tomp architecture

- Kernel: first-level interrupt handler; sequence
  state transition; sequence scheduling; and
  intersequence and interprocessor message-passing.
- IL interpreter: execution of intermediate language
  or system routines generated by the code
  generator.
- Debugging support: breakpoints, tracers,
  enforcements of computational states, and
  interprocessor transfer of debugging commands and
  data.
- Execution control support: monitoring system
  operation and handling emergencies.

      To achieve retargetability of the run-time system,
we are redesigning it in MML with some parts assembly-coded
for efficiency (in particular, the IL interpreter and low-
level mechanisms of the kernel). Kernels for different
architectures will include only the modules required by the
functions to be supported. The structure of the kernel is:

```
what is the architecture ?> TOMP
name your configuration  ?> SYSTEM-1
list processors       NAME        MODEL        IO-MODE
                 (identifier) (Z8001,68000) (io-mapped, or
                                            memory-mapped)
                ?>   P1          Z8001        io-mapped
                ?>   P2          Z8001        io-mapped
                ?>   -
list memory banks    NAME    LENGTH   IN-RIGHTS  WORD-LENGTH
                 (identifier)(0..64K) (rom,ram)    (16)
                ?>   M1       32K        ram        -
                ?>   M12       4K        ram        -
                ?>   M2       32K        ram        -
                ?>   MC        8K        ram        -
                ?>   ...
                ?>   -
list data-links      NAME    SPEED   DIRECTION      CONNECTED
                                                   PROCESSORS
                 (identifier) (high,   (one-way,    (processor
                              med,low)  two-way)      NAME)
                ?>   CH1      high      two-way      P1,P2
                ?>   -
list, for processor P1:
links:           NAME          TYPE
            (identifier)(general-link,data-link,signal-link)
           ?>  LB1          general-link
           ?>  GB1          general-link
           ?>  CH1          data-link
           ?>  S12          signal-link
           ?>  -
memories: LINK  NAME  LOCALITY  RIGHTS   ADDRESS  ACCESS-SPEED
            (id) (private,  (read    (0..64K) (high,med,
      (link NAME)    local,   write,data,          low)
                     global)  stack,...)
       ?>  LB1   M1    private  read-write    0       high
       ?>  LB1   M12   global   read-write   32K      high
       ?>  GB1   MC    global   read-write   56K      low
       ?>  GB1   M12   global   read-write   40K      low
       ?>  GB1   M21   global   read-write   44K      low
       ?>  -
io-devices:LINK  NAME  MODEL  INTERRUPT-ID   PORT-     PORT-
        (general        (pio,sio   (0..64K)   NAMES   ADDRESSES
        link NAME)       ...)                (ids.)   (0..64K)
       ?>  LB1  KEYB      pio      16      data,control  18,20
       ?>  LB1  CH1-INTRF sio       8      data,control  16,14
       ?>  -
processors:     LINK            NAME         INTERFACE-DEVICE
           (data link NAME) (processor NAME) (io-device NAME)
       ?>   CH1              P2               CH1-INTRF
       ?>   -
processor: LINK    NAME   INTERRUPT  SIGNAL-PORT SIGNAL-PORT
     (signal link (processor  -ID       NAME       ADDRESS
        NAME)      NAME)    (0..64K)    (id.)     (0..64K)
       ?>   S12     P2       22       s12-port      38
       ?>   -
list, for processor P1:   <analogous to P1>
```

Figure 9.7 Network description session for the two-processor
prototype in Figure 9.6

```
give prototype configuration name:      ?>   SYSTEM-1
give program name:                      ?>   PRODUCER-CONSUMER
list sequences to be executed by:
    processor P1    ?>      C1, P1
    processor P2    ?>      C2, BUFFER
do you want to choose memory allocation:
    for sequence P1         ?>    no
    for sequence BUFFER     ?>    no
    for sequence C1         ?>    no
    for sequence C2         ?>    yes
list allocation of the modules owned by sequence C2
to memory banks:
    module CONSUMER_CODE  to  ?>   M2
    module CONSUMER2_DATA to  ?>   M21
do you want to allocate private channels to sequences?> yes
list        PRIVATEOWNER_1   PRIVATEOWNER_2   CHANNEL
    ?>          C1              BUFFER          CH1
    ?>          P1              BUFFER          on-memory channel
    ?>          -
```

Figure 9.8 A DPB session for the source program of Figure
9.2 and the target of Figure 9.6

- Level 4: communication via routing of messages
  among processors (not implemented).
- Level 3: communication between sequences allocated
  to directly linked processors.
- Level 2: multisequence scheduling, debugging and
  execution control mechanisms, and communication
  between local sequences.
- Level 1: sequence concept and interleaving
  operations; and first-level interrupt handling.

Debugging.
      Debugging a sequential program is already a
nontrivial job; for concurrent and distributed programs, the
job becomes even more challenging. We propose a four-step
approach in MML:

1) Compilation of programs on the host (a first check
   for syntax and static semantics);
2) Execution of target programs on a host-simulated
   single-processor target;
3) Execution on a reduced target configuration,
   connected to the host that supervises execution;
4) Execution on the complete target configuration in
   the field without the host.

A common core of debugging commands has been
designed for environments (3) and (4); some higher level
commands need support of the host.

We decided it would not be practical to rely on
such special monitoring hardware as in-circuit emulators and
bus inspectors because of our retargetability requirement,
but we do not rule out further developments to take
advantage of specific hardware monitors. As a consequence,
at present, our debugger will not provide continuous real-
time operation.

In a multi-microprocessor target, several parallel
activities have to be monitored and reported to the debugger
operator sitting at the host or at a specific processor of
the target to be called the "entry" processor. Thus, we
assume that the entry processor is directly linked via a
channel to any other processor and to the host when the
target is in the lab.

The main features of the debugging command
language (DCL), include instructions for controlling
execution, for inspecting and modifying variables, for
tracing events, and for making activation of DCL commands
conditional on specified conditions; special care has been
devoted to conditions related to concurrency.

The debugging system requires a DCL interpreter
(host or entry resident) and run-time debugging support,
which can be viewed as an extension of MML kernels. The DCL
interpreter accesses symbolic information originating from
MMDS. If this information is too cumbersome for a stand-
alone entry node, down-graded nonsymbolic references to MML
entities are accepted.

On each target processor, the debugging support
monitors conditions received from the entry and sends
relevant information back to the entry. The traffic of
messages back and forth between entry and other nodes can be
performed by prioritised MML sequences, with the debugging
support in MML with some extension to be target-independent.
The required debugging support is automatically included on
each processor during the network description session.

Execution control and enforcement.

Industrial applications often have stringent
requirements regarding reliability that cannot be met by
traditional programming languages and systems. Multiple
microprocessors, in principle, present favourable
opportunities for achieving high availability and graceful
degradation. The problems to be faced concern error/fault
detection, confinement, and recovery.

After carefully analyzing the innovative features
proposed in some languages, such as recovery blocks and
exception handling, we concluded that they do not provide a
satisfactory or general enough solution to the illspecified
and disparate problems of fault tolerance. In particular,
Ada's difficulties in defining intertask exception handling
constrained us from following that approach.

We propose an execution control and enforcement,
or ECE, level of software that is separately defined and
compiled after application program preparation. We also
refer to ECE programs as "superprograms" that are written by
the user, acting as a "superprogrammer," with full knowledge
of MML programs. Superprograms define and monitor program
events occurring during execution of MML programs and
perform programmed enforcement actions to steer the system
away from error states and back into correct or gracefully
degraded operation.

In some sense, ECE superprograms act as a human
debugging operator, monitoring operations by placing
breakpoints and performing recovery actions. However, unlike

debugging commands, ECE superprograms are permanently
present on the target.

ECE is still under design. It is an open-ended
proposal for providing error detection and exceptions,
checkpointing recovery, and mechanisms for implementing such
known proposals as recovery blocks and triple-modular
redundancy.

Future plans.

The first version of MML was completed at the end
of 1981. The host environment is a PDP-11/34 under RSX. All
tools are coded in OMSI Pascal.

This implementation produces executable programs
for the Z80-based Mimp architecture prototypes (Mezzaline &
Tisato 1979). Experimentation on the MML-programmed Mimp
system is currently going on at the Politecnico di Milano.
The same version also operates for Zeta boards, an
industrial set based on Intel 8085 processors (Zeltron
1982).

A fuller version of MMDS and RTS, including
debugging support, is in progress for 8-bit and 16-bit
architectures, especially Tomp (Conte 1981) and Modiac
(Bertora 1980) boards, the latter a two-level bus
architecture using Z8000 processors. Systems based in the
LSI-11 are also being considered.

Acknowledgement

This work was supported by the Italian National
Research Council, as a part of "Progetto finalizzato per
l'Informatica", under the coordination of A.R.Meo,
U.Montanari and R.Laschi.

The MML project is a joint effort of: CISE
(Segrate), CSISEI (c/o Dip. di Elettronica, Politecnico di
Milano), LMA (c/o Ist. di Matematica, Universita di Genova),
Micromegas (Pisa), Universita di Bologna Ist. di Automatica,
Universita di Pavia Ist. di Informatica e Sistemistica,
Telettra (Bologna), and TXT (Milano), under the management
of A.Dapra` (TXT).

10

Conclusions

Small and medium-sized microcomputer-based distributed systems are becoming more frequently used for control applications (e.g. production automation and quality control). The advantages of a distributed approach over traditional centralised solutions include modularity, fault-tolerance and expandability. To make these benefits available to industry, a suitable language and program development system should be provided. The purpose of Chapter 4 was to examine Ada and the Apse in this respect.

Our analysis of the suitability of the Ada language reached the conclusion that the language meets or exceeds all our requirements (the only notable exception being the absence of static pointers). This means that Ada's expressive power is perfectly suited to our applications. Therefore the only question is one of efficiency: will the greater complexity of Ada compared to other suitable languages cause excessive penalty in terms of host size, target efficiency and ease of learning? We feel that only the last may be a problem.

At present, Ada can only be used to program distributed applications by writing separate programs for each processor. Using Ada in the way we recommend will not be possible for a few years. Eventually, as discussed in section 3.3, Apses should offer substantial advantages over current environments.

We are disappointed that distributed targets have been considered so little, both in the design of the Ada language and in the various Mapse projects.

The crucial aspects of handling distributed targets relate to implementation rather than to language design. The Ada language does not offer suitable facilities and we do not believe that it should. It is the Apse that should bear the burden of preparing programs for distributed targets. Present Apses do not address this problem.

It would be inappropriate to use Ada without any restrictions, for programming distributed systems, notably because Ada allows data to be shared between tasks which might be physically remote. (A similar conclusion would be reached for most languages.)

We have proposed an approach to designing Ada programs for distributed targets that we call the virtual node approach. We believe this to be a natural and desirable way of programming distributed systems; the details of physical configuration are not fixed until the final stages of software construction.

We have studied how the Apse would support this approach. We have proposed a few extra tools and some enhancements to existing tools.

References

ASZ. Manuale d'uso dell'Assembler Strutturato Zeltron.
Zeltron Sistemi Industriali. Specifiche di sistema.
Rapporto n.Z3034.

Allan R. (1979). The microcomputer invades the production line.
IEEE Spectrum, January 1979.

Anderson T., & Lee P.A. (1981). Fault Tolerance : Principles
and Practice. Prentice/Hall International.

Anderson T., and Kerr, R. (1976). Recovery Blocks in action:
a system supporting high reliability.
Proc.Int.Conf Software Engineering.

Andrews G.R. (1981). The distributed programming language SR:
mechanism design and implementation.
Software Practice and Experience., 12, No. 8, 1981.

Bentley J.L., & Shaw M. (1980). *MOD - a language for
distributed programming.
IEEE Trans. SE-6, No. 6, Nov. 1980.

Bertora F., et al. (1980). Sistema Modiac per l'automazione
industriale: architettura del nodo di elaborazione.
Proc. Annual Congress AICA. Italy Oct. 1980.

Boari M., Crespi-Reghizzi S., Dapra' A., & Natali A. (1982a).
How to program multi-microprocessor systems:
survey and experience with MML, a high-level
programming line for industrial applications .
Rapporto MUMICRO 1982.

Boari M., et al. (1982b). MML: a programming line for
multiple-microprocessor systems.
Proceedings of the 3rd International Conference on
Distributed Computing Systems, pp 680-688, Miami, 1982.

Boari M., Crespi-Reghizzi S., Dapra' A., Maderna F., & Natali A.
(1984). Multimicroprocessor programming techniques:
MML, a new set of tools. IEEE Computer, Jan 1984.

Brinch Hansen P. (1975). The programming language
Concurrent Pascal. IEEE Trans. Software Eng,
vol. SE-1, pp. 199-207, June 1975.

Brinch Hansen P. (1978). Distributed processes: a concurrent
programming concept, Comm. ACM, 4, No. 11, 1978.

Brinch Hansen P. (1981). Edison - A Multiprocessor Language,
Software Practice and Experience.
vol. 11, no.4, pp. 325-397, April 1981.

Chen L., & Avizienis A. (1978). N-Version Programming :
A Fault Tolerance Approach to Reliability of Software
Operation. Digest of Papers FTCS-8: Eighth Annual
International Conference on Fault-Tolerant Computing,
Toulouse, 3-9.

Conte G., et al (1981).
TOMP 80: A multi-microprocessor prototype.
Euromicro 81 Symposium, North Holland.

Conway R., Gries D., Fay M., & Bass C. (1979).
        Introduction to microprocessor programming using PLZ.
        Winthrop Publishers, Inc. Cambridge, Massachussets.
Crespi-Reghizzi S., Corti P., & Dapra' A. (1980). A Survey of
        Microprocessor Languages. IEEE Computer, January 1980.
DOD (1978). "Ironman" : Requirements for high order computer
        programming languages. Defense Advanced Research
        Projects Agency, Arlington, June 1978.
DOD (1980). "Stoneman" : Requirements for Ada programming
        support environments.
        U.S. Dept. of Defense, Feb. 1980.
DOD (1983). "LRM". Reference Manual for the Ada Programming
        Language. ANSI/MIL-STD-1815A. US DOD. Jan 1983.
DOD (1984). Draft Specification of the Common Apse Interface
        Set (CAIS). Version 1.2. 31 May 1984. AJPO.
Downes V.A., & Goldsack S.J. (1980). The use of the Ada
        language for programming a distributed system.
        Real-time Programming Work-shop, Graz, April 1980.
Droz P.H., & Jansson H. (1981).
        Micro-Concurrent Pascal suits real-time applications.
        Electronic Designer, pp. 117-122, May 1981.
Ghezzi C., Tisato F. & Viola E. (1982). X - CODE: the
        visibility in Ada of the X - CODE abstract machine.
        CNR CNET Series, No. 81, 1982.
Glanville R.S., & Graham S.L. (1977). A new method for
        compiler code generation. Proc. Fifth ACM Symp. on
        Principles of Programming Languages.
Habermann A.N., & Nassi I.R. (1980). Efficient implementation
        of Ada tasks, Dept. of Computer Science,
        Carnegie-Mellon University, CMU-CS-80-103.
Hoare C.A.R. (1974).
        Monitors: an operating system structuring concept.
        Comm ACM, vol. 14, p. 549, Oct. 1974.
Hoare C.A.R. (1978). Communicating Sequential Processes.
        CACM, 21, no. 8, 666-677.
Hoare C.A.R. (1981). The Emperor's New Clothes.
        CACM, 24, no. 2, 75-83.
Hopkins A.L. (1980). Fault-tolerant system design:
        broadbrush and fine points.
        IEEE Computer, 13, 3, 39-46.
Horning, J.J. et al. (1974). A program structure for error
        detection and recovery.
        Springer-Verlag, Lecture notes in Comp. Sci.,
        Vol 16, pp. 177-193.
Hull R., Halsall F. & Grimsdale R.L. (1983).
        The Virtual Resource Ring : A Technique for
        Decentralized Resource Management in Fault Tolerant
        Distributed Computer Systems.
        To appear in IEE Proceedings, Part E.
Intel (1977a). PLM/80 Programming Manual.
Intel (1977b). RMX/80 User's guide.
Intermetrics (1982). Computer Program Development
        Specification for the Ada Integrated Environment.
        B5 Specifications. Intermetrics Inc. Nov 1982.
Inveradi P., Montanari U., & Vallario G. (1982).
        How to program an Apse (almost) completely in Ada.
        Report 68, project CNET, ETS, Pisa.

Jessop K.H. (1982). Ada packages and distributed systems,
        ACM Sigplan Notices, 1982.
Kramer J., Magee J., Sloman M. & Lister A. (1983).
        CONIC: An Integrated Approach to Distributed
        Computer Control Systems. IEE Proceedings,
        13Ø, Part E, no. 1, January 1983.
Lee, P.A. et al. (198Ø) A recovery cache for the PDP-11.
        IEEE Trans. on Comp., C-29(6), 546, June 198Ø
Liskov B. (1982).
        On linguistic support for distributed programs.
        IEEE Trans. SE-8, No. 3, May 1982.
Liskov B. (1984). The ARGUS language and system.
        In Advanced Course on Distributed Systems.
        Munich. April 1984.
Lomet, D.B., (1977) Process structuring, synchronisation
        and recovery using atomic actions. Proc. ACM
        Conf. on Language Design for Reliable Software,
        SIGPLAN Notices, 12, 3, March 1977, 128-137.
Magee J. & Kramer J. (1983). Dynamic System Configuration
        for Distributed Real-Time Systems.
        IFAC/IFIP Workshop on Real-Time Programming.
        Hatfield, March 1983.
Martin T. (1977). PEARL at the Age of Five.
        Proceedings of the 4th Software Engineering
        Conference, (Munich 1977). IEEE.
Mezzalira L., & Tisato F. (1979). An approach to Modular
        Multicomputer Systems. Euromicro 1979.
Olivetti (1982). Portable Ada Programming System, Global
        Design Report, January 1982;
        Olivetti Gruppo Informatica Distribuita.
Randell B., Lee P.A., & Treleaven P.C. (1978),
        Reliability Issues in Computing System Design.
        ACM Computing Surveys, 1Ø no.2.
Randell, B., (1975).
        System structure for Software Fault Tolerance.
        IEEE Trans. Software Eng., Vol SE-1, June 1975.
Rennels D.A. (198Ø). Distributed fault-tolerant computer
        systems. IEEE Computer 13, 3, 55-66.
Rossi G., & Zicari R. (1982). Un primo approccio alla
        programmazione distribuita con ADA,
        Dipt. Elettronica, Politecnico di Milano, June 1982.
SPL (198Ø). RTL/2 Training Manual. RTL/2 Ref 3, version 2.
        SPL International, Abingdon, UK.
SPL, SDL, SSL, & ICL (1981). UK Ada Study : Final Technical
        Report, June 1981. Available from the Librarian,
        Division of Numerical Analysis and Computer
        Science. NPL, Teddington, Middlesex, England.
Shoja G.C. et al. (1982). A control kernel to support Ada
        intertask communication on a distributed
        multiprocessor computer system,
        Software and Microsystems, 1, No. 5, Aug. 1982.
Softech (1982).
        ALS Kapse - B5 Specification. Softech, Feb 1982.
TXT, CISE, & SPL International, (1983).
        A feasibility study to determine the applicability
        of Ada and Apse in a multi-microprocessor
        distributed environment. March 1983.

Wensley J.H., Levitt K.N. & Newmann P.G. (1974).
        A Comparative Study of Architectures for Fault
        Tolerance.   Proceedings 4th International Symposium
        on Fault-Tolerant Computing, pp. 4-21, IEEE, 1974.
Wirth N. (1977). Modula: a language for modular
        multiprogramming. Software practice and experience,
        vol. 7 pp. 3-35, 1977.
Zeltron. Manuale d'uso di ZEX : Zeltron Executive.
        Zeltron Sistemi Industriali. Specifiche di sistema.
        Rapporto n.Z3403.
Zeltron (1982).   Zeta Modules User manual. Zeltron Automazione.